THE ENCYCLOPEDIA OF PSYCHOACTIVE DRUGS

IN 25 VOLUMES
Each title on a specific drug or drug-related problem

LSD

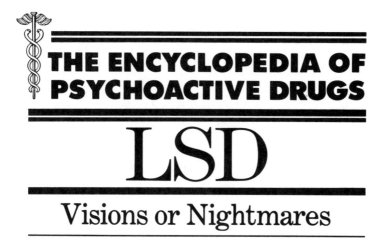

THE ENCYCLOPEDIA OF PSYCHOACTIVE DRUGS

LSD

Visions or Nightmares

MICHAEL E. TRULSON, Ph.D.

Texas A & M University College of Medicine

GENERAL EDITOR
Professor Solomon H. Snyder, M.D.

*Distinguished Service Professor of
Neuroscience, Pharmacology, and Psychiatry at
The John Hopkins University School of Medicine*

ASSOCIATE EDITOR
Professor Barry L. Jacobs, Ph.D.

Program in Neuroscience, Department of Psychology, Princeton University

SENIOR EDITORIAL CONSULTANT
Jerome H. Jaffe, M.D.

Director of The Addiction Research Center, National Institute on Drug Abuse

1985
CHELSEA HOUSE PUBLISHERS
NEW YORK

MANAGING EDITOR: William P. Hansen
ASSOCIATE EDITORS: John Haney, Richard Mandell
CAPTIONS EDITOR: Richard Mandell
EDITORIAL COORDINATOR: Karyn Gullen Browne
ART DIRECTOR: Susan Lusk
LAYOUT: Carol McDougall
ART ASSISTANT : Teresa Clark
PICTURE RESEARCH: Susan Quist

First Printing

Library of Congress Cataloging in Publication Data
Trulson, Michael
  LSD: visions or nightmares
  (The Encyclopedia of psychoactive drugs)
  1. Lysergic acid diethylamide. I. Title
II. Title: L.S.D. III. Series
BF209.L9T78   1984   615'.7883   84-14936

ISBN 0-87754-752-1

Chelsea House Publishers
Harold Steinberg, Chairman & Publisher
Susan Lusk, Vice President
A Division of Chelsea House Educational Communications, Inc.

Chelsea House Publishers
133 Christopher Street
New York, NY 10014

Photos courtesy of AP/Wide World Photos, Ivan Albright, Richard Aldcroft,
Michael Alexander, Eugene Anthony, Richard Avedon, Harriet Francis, Rick
Griffin, *High Times* magazine, Albert Hofmann, *New York Times,* Pavel
Tchelitchew, U.S. Drug Enforcement Administration, United Press
International, and Yando.

CONTENTS

In the 1960s the youth of America, hungry for social and political change and inspired by LSD and other drugs, came together at rallies, Be-Ins, Love-Ins, and rock concerts.

FOREWORD

In the Mainstream of American Life

The rapid growth of drug use and abuse is one of the most dramatic changes in the fabric of American society in the last 20 years. The United States has the highest level of psychoactive drug use of any industrialized society. It is 10 to 30 times greater than it was 20 years ago.

According to a recent Gallup poll, young people consider drugs the leading problem that they face. One of the legacies of the social upheaval of the 1960s is that psychoactive drugs have become part of the mainstream of American life. Schools, homes, and communities cannot be "drug proofed." There is a demand for drugs—and the supply is plentiful. Social norms have changed and drugs are not only available—they are everywhere.

Almost all drug use begins in the preteen and teenage years. These years are few in the total life cycle, but critical in the maturation process. During these years adolescents face the difficult tasks of discovering their identity, clarifying their sexual roles, asserting their independence, learning to cope with authority, and searching for goals that will give their lives meaning. During this intense period of growth, conflict is inevitable and the temptation to use drugs is great. Drugs are readily available, adolescents are curious and vulnerable, there is peer pressure to experiment, and there is the temptation to escape from conflicts.

No matter what their age or socioeconomic status, no group is immune to the allure and effects of psychoactive drugs. The U.S. Surgeon General's report, "Healthy People," indicates that 30% of all deaths in the United States

Unable to cope with the stress and intensity of LSD, 19-year-old Craig Gardner recorded his will and his struggle with LSD, then shot himself.

are premature because of alcohol and tobacco use. However, the most shocking development in this report is that mortality in the age group between 15 and 24 has increased since 1960 despite the fact that death rates for all other age groups have declined in the 20th century. Accidents, suicides and homicides are the leading cause of death in young people 15 to 24 years of age. In many cases the deaths are directly related to drug use.

THE ENCYCLOPEDIA OF PSYCHOACTIVE DRUGS answers the questions that young people are likely to ask about drugs, as well as those they might not think to ask, but should. Topics include: what it means to be intoxicated; how drugs affect mood; why people take drugs; who takes them; when they take them; and how much they take. They will learn what happens to a drug when it enters the body. They will learn what it means to get "hooked" and how it happens. They will learn how drugs affect their driving, their school work, and those around them—their peers, their family, their friends, and their employers. They will learn what the signs are that indicate that a friend or a family member may have a drug problem and to identify four stages leading from drug use to drug abuse. Myths about drugs are dispelled.

National surveys indicate that students are eager for information about drugs and that they respond to it. Students not only need information about drugs—they want information. How they get it often proves crucial. Providing young people with accurate knowledge about drugs is one of the most critical aspects.

THE ENCYCLOPEDIA OF PSYCHOACTIVE DRUGS synthesizes the wealth of new information in this field and demystifies this complex and important subject. Each volume in the series is written by an expert in the field. Handsomely illustrated, this multi-volume series is geared for teenage readers. Young people will read these books, share them, talk about them, and make more informed decisions because of them.

Miriam Cohen
Contributing Editor

A poster by Rick Griffin, advertising the Human Be-In on January 14, 1967, at Golden Gate Park in San Francisco. A gathering of "Tribes" which was to bring together more than 3000, the event celebrated the humanization of America, with the hope that it would mark the beginning of a renaissance of compassion, awareness, and love.

INTRODUCTION

The Gift of Wizardry
Use and Abuse

Jack H. Mendelson, M.D.
Nancy K. Mello, Ph.D.
Alcohol and Drug Abuse Research Center
Harvard Medical School—McLean Hospital

Dorothy to the Wizard:

"I think you are a very bad man," said Dorothy.
"Oh, no, my dear; I'm really a very good man; but I'm a very bad Wizard."
—from THE WIZARD OF OZ

Man is endowed with the gift of wizardry, a talent for discovery and invention. The discovery and invention of substances that change the way we feel and behave are among man's special accomplishments, and like so many other products of our wizardry, these substances have the capacity to harm as well as to help. The substance itself is neutral, an intricate molecular structure. Yet, "too much" can be sickening, even deadly. It is man who decides how each substance is used, and it is man's beliefs and perceptions that give this neutral substance the attributes to heal or destroy.

Consider alcohol—available to all and yet regarded with intense ambivalence from biblical times to the present day. The use of alcoholic beverages dates back to our earliest ancestors. Alcohol use and misuse became associated with the worship of gods and demons. One of the most powerful Greek gods was Dionysus, lord of the Underworld and god of wine. The Romans adopted Dionysus but changed his name to Bacchus. Festivals and holidays associated with Bacchus celebrated the harvest and the origins of life. Time has blurred the images of the Bacchanalian festival, but the theme of drunkenness as a major part of celebration has survived the pagan gods and remains a familiar part of modern society. The term "Bacchanalian festival" conveys a more appealing image than "drunken orgy" or "pot party," but whatever the label, some of the celebrants will inevitably start up the "high" escalator to the next plateau. Once there, the de-escalation is difficult for many.

According to reliable estimates, one out of every ten Americans develops a serious alcohol-related problem sometime in his or her lifetime. In addition, automobile accidents caused by drunken drivers claim the lives of tens of thousands every year. Many of the victims are gifted young people, just starting out in adult life. Hospital emergency rooms abound with patients seeking help for alcohol-related injuries.

Who is to blame? Can we blame the many manufacturers who produce such an amazing variety of alcoholic beverages? Should we blame the educators who fail to explain the perils of intoxication, or so exaggerate the dangers of drinking that no one could possibly believe them? Are friends to blame—those peers who urge others to "drink more and faster," or the macho types who stress the importance of being able to "hold your liquor"? Casting blame, however, is hardly constructive, and pointing the finger is a fruitless way to deal with problems. Alcoholism and drug abuse have few culprits but many victims. Accountability begins with each of us, every time we choose to use or to misuse an intoxicating substance.

It is ironic that some of man's earliest medicines, derived from natural plant products, are used today to poison and to intoxicate. Relief from pain and suffering is one of society's many continuing goals. Over 3,000 years ago, the Therapeutic Papyrus of Thebes, one of our earliest written records, gave instructions for the use of opium in the treatment of pain. Opium, in the form of its major derivative, morphine, remains one of the most powerful drugs we have for pain relief. But opium, morphine, and similar compounds, such as heroin, have also been used by many to induce changes in mood and feeling. Another example of man's misuse of a natural substance is the coca leaf, which for centuries was used by the Indians of Peru to reduce fatigue and hunger. Its modern derivative, cocaine, has important medical use as a local anesthetic. Unfortunately, its increasing abuse in the 1980s has reached epidemic proportions.

The purpose of this series is to provide information about the nature and behavioral effects of alcohol and drugs, and the probable consequences of both their moderate use and abuse. The authors believe that up-to-date, objective information about alcohol and drugs will help readers make better decisions as to whether to use them or not. The information presented here (and in other books in this series) is based on many clinical and laboratory studies and observations by people from diverse walks of life.

Over the centuries, novelists, poets, and dramatists have provided us with many insights into the beneficial and problematic aspects of alcohol and drug use. Physicians, lawyers, biologists, psychologists, and social scientists have contributed to a better understanding of the causes and consequences of using these substances. The authors in this series have attempted to gather and condense all the latest information about drug use and abuse. They have also described the sometimes wide gaps in our knowledge and have suggested some new ways to answer many difficult questions.

One such question, for example, is how do alcohol and drug problems get started? And what is the best way to treat them when they do? Not too many years ago, alcoholics and drug abusers were regarded as evil, immoral, or both. It is now recognized that these persons suffer from very complicated diseases involving deep psychological and social problems. To understand how the disease begins and progresses, it is necessary to understand the nature of the substance, the behavior of the afflicted person, and the characteristics of the society or culture in which he lives.

The diagram below shows the interaction of these three factors. The arrows indicate that the substance not only affects the user personally, but the society as well. Society influences attitudes towards the substance, which in turn affect its availability. The substance's impact upon the society may support or discourage the use and abuse of that substance.

SUBSTANCE
(ALCOHOL OR DRUG)

PERSON ⟷ SOCIETY

The Garden of Earthly Delights *painted by Hieronymus Bosch around 1500. Though not induced by LSD, Bosch's paintings depict the pessimism and disillusionment with society sometimes experienced during a bad trip.*

Although many of the social environments we live in are very similar, some of the most subtle differences can strongly influence our thinking and behavior. Where we live, go to school and work, whom we discuss things with—all influence our opinions about drug use and misuse. Yet we also share certain commonly accepted beliefs that outweigh any differences in our attitudes. The authors in this series have tried to identify and discuss the central, most crucial issues concerning drug use and misuse.

Regrettably, man's wizardry in developing new substances in medical therapeutics has not always been paralleled by intelligent usage. Although we do know a great deal about the effects of alcohol and drugs, we have yet to learn how to impart that knowledge, especially to young adults.

Does it matter? What harm does it do to smoke a little pot or have a few beers? What is it like to be intoxicated? How long does it last? Will it make me feel really fine? Will it make me sick? What are the risks? These are but a few of the questions answered in this series, which, hopefully, will enable the reader to make wise decisions concerning the crucial issue of drugs.

Information sensibly acted upon can go a long way towards helping everyone develop his or her best self. As one keen and sensitive observer, Dr. Lewis Thomas, has said,

> "There is nothing at all absurd about the human condition. We matter. It seems to me a good guess, hazarded by a good many people who have thought about it, that we may be engaged in the formation of something like a mind for the life of this planet. If this is so, we are still at the most primitive stage, still fumbling with language and thinking, but infinitely capacitated for the future. Looked at this way, it is remarkable that we've come as far as we have in so short a period, really no time at all as geologists measure time. We are the newest, the youngest, and the brightest thing around."

Ergot, shown above growing on rye, is a dark fungus which contains the "skeleton" for synthesizing LSD. This may have been used by the Greeks 2000 years ago in their annual initiation into the Mysteries of Eleusis, honoring the god Dionysus.

CHAPTER 1

DISCOVERY AND USES OF LSD

LSD was first produced in 1938 by Dr. Albert Hofmann, a Swiss chemist seeking to synthesize a new drug for the treatment of headache. Dr. Hofmann obtained lysergic acid from the ergot fungus, a parasite which grows on the rye plant. From lysergic acid he synthesized the compound lysergic acid diethlyamide (LSD). He tested it in laboratory animals for its analgesic (pain-killing) properties using standard procedures. Since it appeared to be totally inactive, the bottle of LSD was placed on a shelf in Dr. Hofmann's laboratory, where it remained untouched for five years. Little did Hofmann know that he had produced the most potent psychoactive drug ever known, or that the newly synthesized drug would have an impact on society some 25 years later.

On April 16, 1943, Hofmann decided to do some further testing with LSD. In handling the drug, he accidentally ingested an unknown quantity. His personal account of the drug's effects was remarkably accurate and virtually everything he described has been confirmed by subsequent studies. His journal contains this dramatic entry:

> *Last Friday, April 16, 1943, I was forced to stop my work in the laboratory in the middle of the afternoon and to go home, as I was seized by a pecu-*

liar restlessness associated with a sensation of mild dizziness. Having reached home, I lay down and sank in a kind of drunkness which was not unpleasant and which was characterized by extreme activity of imagination. As I lay in a dazed condition with my eyes closed (I experienced daylight as disagreeably bright) there surged upon me an uninterrupted stream of fantastic images of extraordinary plasticity and vividness and accompanied by an intense, kaleidoscope-like play of colors. This condition gradually passed off after about two hours.

Three days later, in an attempt to verify that the episode was indeed caused by the ingestion of LSD, Hofmann took what he thought would be a small quantity of the drug, 250 micrograms (1 microgram = 1/1,000,000 grams). This is approximately five times the dose necessary to produce intense hallucinations in an average adult male. Therefore, the drug-induced effects were much more intense than the first time Dr. Hofmann ingested LSD. Approximately 40 minutes after taking the drug, Hofmann noted that he felt unrest, dizziness, visual disturbances, a tendency to laugh at inappropriate times, and difficulty in concentration. His journal reads:

Here stop the laboratory notes. The last words can be written only with great effort. I asked my lab helper to accompany me home, since I believed the process would take the same course as the disturbance on the Friday before. However, already on

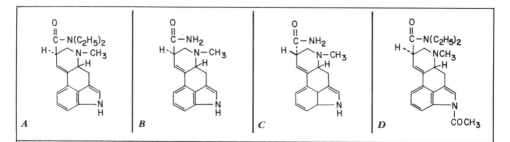

Figure A shows the chemical structure of LSD. B and C represent the psychoactive agents in Hawaiian woodroses and some morning glories. D is a popular form of LSD. Note the similar four rings in each one.

the bicycle ride home it was clear that all symptoms were more intense than the first time. I already had great trouble speaking clearly and my field of vision wavered and was distorted as a picture in a curved mirror. Also I had the feeling of not leaving the spot whereas my lab helper later told me we had traveled at a brisk pace. So far as I can remember, the following symptoms were most pronounced during the height of the crisis and before the physician came: dizziness, visual disturbances; the faces of those present appeared to me as colored grimaces; strong motor unrest alternating with paralysis; the head, the entire body and all of the limbs appeared at times heavy as if filled with metal; cramps in the calves, hands at times numb, cold; a

Dr. Albert Hofmann holding a model of LSD-25, the drug which he first synthesized in 1943 while creating new compounds from ergot. Several of these proved useful in medicine—in obstetrics, in geriatrics, and in the treatment of migraine headaches. However, the 25th compound, LSD-25, did not appear to be of medical value. But when a single drop of this potent compound fell onto his finger Hofmann was the first known person to experience an LSD trip.

metallic taste on the tongue; throat dry, constricted; a feeling of suffocation; alternately stupefied then again clearly aware of the situation, noting as though I were a neutral observer, standing outside myself, that I shouted half crazily or chattered unintelligibly.

Dr. Hofmann's condition was considerably improved six hours after taking the drug, although there were still prominent signs of LSD intoxication, as his journal reveals:

The visual disturbances were still pronounced. Everything appeared to waver; and proportions were distorted, similar to a reflection in moving water. In addition, everything was drenched in changing colors of disagreeable, predominantly poisonous green and blue hues. Colorful, very plastic and fantastic images passed before my closed eyes. It was especially noteworthy that all acoustical perceptions, perchance the noise of a passing car, were

An extract from Dr. Hofmann's laboratory journal describing the preparation of LSD and the first human experiment, using himself. Soon after ingestion Hofmann was unable to continue recording his observations.

translated into optical sensations, so that through each tone and noise, a corresponding colored picture, kaleidoscopically changing in form and color, was elicited.

LSD was first shipped to the United States in 1949. American scientists, eager to learn more about this exotic drug, fed LSD to spiders, fish, rats, cats, dogs, goats, and even a three-ton elephant! It produced dramatic behavioral changes in all species of animals investigated.

A Search for the Therapeutic Value of LSD

During the 1950s, experimentation on the effects of LSD on humans began. There were few restrictions on the use of human "guinea pigs" at this time, and scientists were free to administer the drug widely, hoping to find some useful therapeutic (medical) value for the drug. Because of the dramatic psychic effects of LSD, and Hofmann's account of the depersonalization produced by the drug, most early

a

b

Drawings created before (a) and during (b) an LSD trip experienced by a neurotic, college-educated man during a psychological study. He described the pretest drawings as a young salesman carrying a briefcase, and a female wearing a bathingsuit, a "bathing ugly." The LSD drawings were of a "sly, tricky old man" and a 75-year old woman, "kindly, generous, pleasant and proper." The results suggest that LSD weakened his defenses and brought out his autistic, paranoid thinking.

studies were aimed at utilizing the drug to treat various psychiatric disorders. It was felt that if the person could "step outside" himself and view his situation as others saw him, he would come to grips with his problems and be better able to solve them. One of the first major areas of research with LSD was in treating alcoholism. It was hoped that LSD, by its depersonalizing effect, would allow the alcoholic to look at his illness more objectively and gain insight into the reasons for, and the results of, his drinking habits. After extensive experimentation, however, it was concluded that LSD was not effective in treating alcoholics, and this line of research was discontinued.

LSD was also tested on schizophrenics, narcotic addicts, sexually maladjusted people, and criminals, again with the hope that the individual could learn to view his behavior objectively. This, in turn, would make the process of rehabilitation much easier. Unfortunately, research determined that LSD was not effective in treating any of these conditions. Despite its depersonalizing effect, the drug was found inef-

Actor Cary Grant was one of 110 patients, including his wife and several other Hollywood actors, who participated in an experimental LSD therapy program. After stories of the LSD experiences received publicity, nonparticipating psychiatrists complained that their patients were begging for LSD.

fective in treating any sort of behavioral problem. Even worse, it was becoming apparent that LSD may transform a normal individual into a person with a mild to severe personality problem.

LSD has also been used in patients with terminal diseases, such as certain cancers. These patients frequently experience persistent pain which cannot be effectively treated with traditional pain-relieving drugs such as morphine. Remember that Dr. Hofmann developed LSD while searching for new pain-relieving drugs, but that LSD had no such effects in animal laboratory tests. Terminally ill patients have been reported to derive some relief from pain after taking LSD. It is not known, however, whether this is an effect on the pain process itself or whether the drug alters the perception of pain. The hallucinations that occur after taking LSD may simply take the patient's mind off the pain so that he is not as aware of it. This is the most likely explanation. LSD has never been approved by the Food and Drug Administration (FDA) for any therapeutic use, and the drug remains today a "Schedule One Drug"—or one available for research only.

LSD Tested for "Mind Control"

The Central Intelligence Agency (CIA) and various military agencies also became interested in research with LSD in the 1950s. Their interest in such a potent psychoactive drug was in the area of mind control. They saw the possibilities of

In 1976 Kenneth Loebb, who suffered 28 seizures in 19 years, finally persuaded the army to admit that he was secretly given LSD during tests in 1957. LSD, tested on American soldiers, was advocated by the CIA and the army as a way to conduct "humane warfare," since a disoriented enemy would prove easier to disarm.

manipulating the beliefs of even very strong-willed people. They gave LSD to a group of army scientists and then attempted to change some of their basic beliefs while they were under the influence of the drug. However, one of the scientists became psychotic (that is, lost control of his thoughts and actions) under the influence of the drug and jumped to his death from a hotel window. Undaunted, these agencies then used unsuspecting drug addicts and prostitutes to test their mind control theories. After extensive experimentation, it became apparent that the human mind is too complex to be controlled even by a potent drug like LSD. Research along these lines has been discontinued in the United States.

LSD as a Recreational Drug

In 1960 LSD was still strictly confined to the research laboratory. The drug was not part of the drug culture. This

President Ford, on behalf of the U.S. government, apologizes to the family of Dr. Frank Olson. As part of an experiment, Olson, a specialist in chemical weapons, was secretly given LSD. Falsely believing he had revealed important secrets while under the influence of LSD, Dr. Olson jumped from a 10th-floor window and fell to his death.

would all change dramatically within the next few years, largely as the result of one man. That man was Dr. Timothy Leary, an assistant professor of psychology at Harvard University. Dr. Leary was a well-respected, non-controversial clinical psychologist who had taught at Harvard for several years and had co-authored several textbooks. In the early 1960s Dr. Leary experimented with psilocybin, an LSD-like drug, while on a trip to Mexico. Leary was impressed by the drug's ability to produce dramatic perceptual and behavioral effects. He began experimenting with LSD and related drugs, using as his subjects prisoners at a Massachusetts prison.

Though for eight years Timothy Leary had often ingested LSD, an analysis of 200 of his cells showed only two chromosome aberrations.

Through his own use of LSD and observation of convicts given the drug, Leary became convinced that LSD was capable of "expanding consciousness." Dr. Leary began holding sessions with students, in which everyone would take LSD and relate their drug-induced experiences to one another. Dr. Leary openly promoted the use of LSD for the purpose of expanding one's consciousness. Leary and another Harvard University professor, Dr. Richard Alpert, established the International Federation for Internal Freedom (IFIF). They increased their promotional activities of LSD, insisting that these drugs could "recircuit" the brain to produce a more effective and creative organ. Their beliefs gained widespread publicity, as indicated by the following account in *The New York Times*:

> *Dr.'s Alpert and Leary described the changes produced in the mind by the 'consciousness-expanding' drug as similar to those produced in the mind by the printed word or by the power of suggestion. They said that there was no factual evidence that consciousness-expanding drugs are uniquely dangerous and considerable evidence that they are safe and beneficial.*
>
> *They said in their letter to the student newspaper that "there is no reason to believe that consciousness-*

On May 28, 1963, Dr. Nathan M. Pusey, president of Harvard University fired Richard Alpert and Timothy Leary, professors of clinical psychology, stating that, against university policy, they had involved undergraduates in drug experiments.

experiences are any more dangerous than psycho-analysis or a four-year enrollment in Harvard College."

Drs. Leary and Alpert were fired by Harvard in 1963 for their involvement with LSD. They moved to Mexico but were soon asked to leave that country by Mexican authorities. The activities of the two men in promoting the use of LSD, their dismissal from Harvard, and then their expulsion from Mexico received considerable attention throughout the United States. Despite these problems, Leary intensified his crusade to promote the use of LSD. Major magazines, newspapers, and network television did feature stories on Leary and the drug. The widespread publicity accelerated the underground movement to expand the use of LSD and related drugs, and

On January 14, 1967, Timothy Leary told a crowd of thousands of San Francisco hippies to "Turn On, Tune In, and Drop Out."

by the mid-1960s individuals from all walks of life were experimenting with LSD.

At the same time laws were being passed making the manufacture, sale, use, or possession of LSD a crime. The maximum sentence for possession of LSD for first-time offenders was a $5,000 fine and one year in jail. Repeat offenders could be punished with a $100,000 fine and ten years in prison. Sandoz Pharmaceutical Company, the only legal American supplier of LSD, stopped distributing the drug in 1966 and transferred its total supply to the National Institutes of Health, which is the only legal source of LSD.

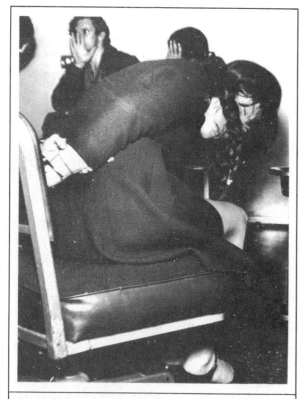

In 1967 Sanna Pinching and other youths were arrested for possession of $500,000 worth of LSD. In the trunk of their car police also found a suitcase which contained $25,000 in cash.

August Owsley Stanley III, the "King of Acid," being arrested and charged with illegal manufacture of a controlled drug.

How Many People Use LSD?

The use of LSD and related hallucinogens continued to increase during the late 1960s and early 1970s, due in part to the publicity received by Leary but also due to the social upheaval that shook the United States during this period. Use of LSD peaked in the late 1960s and then began a steady decline. This decline can be attributed to three factors. First of all, an increasing number of bad trips were reported, and this became widespread knowledge among the members of the underground drug culture. Secondly, a report appeared in 1967 stating that LSD causes chromosomal damage. Finally, other chemicals became the drugs of choice for many users. Mescaline, DOM, and psilocin all became more prevelant around 1970.

By the late 1970s, LSD use had declined even further as many drug users turned to marijuana, phencyclidine (angel dust), cocaine, and heroin, or experimented with drug habits involving volatile solvents (glue-sniffing). While these other drugs are still in widespread use, the early 1980s have seen a resurgence in the use of LSD. We can only speculate

Alfred W. Trembly, captain of the Los Angeles Police Department, claimed in 1966 that the use of LSD had mushroomed into a serious problem.

as to the reasons. For one thing LSD is relatively easy to manufacture in a pure form, compared to drugs such as cocaine and heroin, which are usually smuggled into the country at considerable risk. Also, many of the fears of damage to chromosomes by LSD have been lessened by more recent research which questions earlier findings. Finally, the price of LSD is relatively low, especially in comparison with cocaine and heroin. Whatever the reason, it is clear that LSD is being used more and more frequently in the 1980s than it was in recent years. This makes education concerning its effects and toxicity of great importance for today's society.

A survey taken in 1982 revealed that 5% of students between the ages of 12 and 17 years had experimented with one or more hallucinogens while 21% of young adults (ages 18 to 25 years) had tried at least one hallucinogen and 2% of adults over 35 years of age had tried one or more hallucinogenic drugs at some time during their lives. The statistics for the 35-and-older group is somewhat surprising since they represent many people who were in their late teens and 20s during the 1960s when LSD was in its heyday. It is important to remember that any survey study depends upon the self-report of the individuals and many, particularly older, established individuals, are reluctant to admit to past drug use. Most people who had experimented with hallucinogens reported using them a total of 10 times or less. It was also reported that marijuana is frequently taken at the same time as LSD.

A closer look at the information gathered from high school students in 1982 revealed that 10% of the students had experimented with LSD at some time during their life,

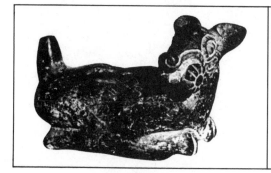

A 2500-year-old ceramic snuffing pipe in the form of a deer with a peyote cactus in its mouth. Found in Oaxaca, Mexico, this artifact strengthens the theory that peyote was a central part of early Mexican culture.

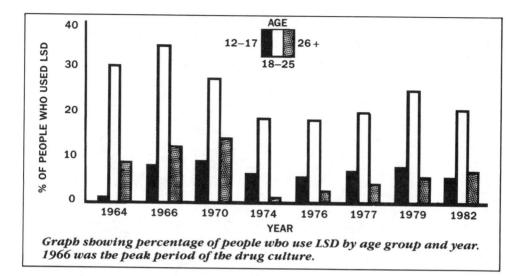

Graph showing percentage of people who use LSD by age group and year. 1966 was the peak period of the drug culture.

6% had used LSD during the past year, and 3% of the seniors had used the drug during the past month. More college-bound students had used LSD than students not planning to attend college, and more men than women had used the drug.

Between 1975 and 1982 there was a 2% decrease in the number of high school seniors who had experimented with LSD. In a survey of parental and peer attitudes towards the use of LSD, 97% of the seniors surveyed reported that their parents would strongly disapprove of their experimenting with LSD, and 88% said that their friends would disapprove. While a small fraction of the total student population actually used LSD, 34% of the senior class of 1982 said that it would be easy for them to obtain the drug.

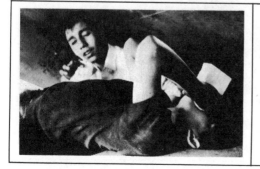

As LSD use declined in the mid-1970s, glue sniffing became popular as a legal and inexpensive means of intoxication. Scientific evidence indicates that this harmful behavior damages the heart, kidneys, liver, and brain.

A micrograph of LSD crystals. A slight change in the chemical structure of LSD renders it inactive. Even the mirror image, in which the molecular structure is reversed, produces no psychoactive effects.

CHAPTER 2

HALLUCINOGENS: WHAT THEY ARE

LSD (lysergic acid diethylamide) is a synthetic drug. That is, it is not found in nature, but rather, is produced in the chemist's laboratory. Drugs similar to LSD in their chemical structure and psychological effects, however, are found in nature. The most common of these is ololiuqui, a vine-like plant that contains a lysergic acid derivative similar to LSD. The ancient Aztecs were aware of the hallucinogenic effects of this plant and used it in religious ceremonies. After consuming the plant, the native priests felt that they were able to communicate with their gods and receive messages from them. These, of course, were hallucinogenic experiences induced by the LSD-like drug in the ololiuqui plant. It is worth pointing out that, while this plant produces hallucinations, it is not nearly as potent as the synthetic compound LSD. In fact, LSD is one of the most potent (that is, a small dose produces a big effect) psychoactive drugs (that is, a drug altering mood and thought processes) known to mankind.

Today, nearly a half-century after LSD was first produced, scientists still have differing opinions on how to classify it. Most prefer the term hallucinogen, which simply means "the perception of objects with no reality," or "the experi-

35

ence of sensations with no external cause." While this is the major effect of LSD, the drug is known to produce a number of other psychological and physiological effects. Therefore, other scientists have used the terms "psychotomimetic" (producing psychotic-like states), "phantasticum" or "delusion-ogen" (indicating that objects are perceived differently than they really are), or "psychedelic" (indicating "mind-altering" or "mind-expanding" properties).

Although scientists have not yet agreed upon a single term to define the actions of LSD on human psychological processes, the term hallucinogen will be used here since it has become the most common. The reader should keep in mind, however, that the terms phantasticum, delusionogen, and psychedelic are frequently used interchangeably.

Drugs that Are Similar to LSD

In addition to LSD, several other drugs are also classified as hallucinogens. Some are frequently referred to as "LSD-like" drugs to distinguish them from other categories of drugs that produce somewhat similar effects. The second most potent LSD-like drug is STP, also known as DOM. STP stands for "serenity, tranquility, and peace," states of mind which

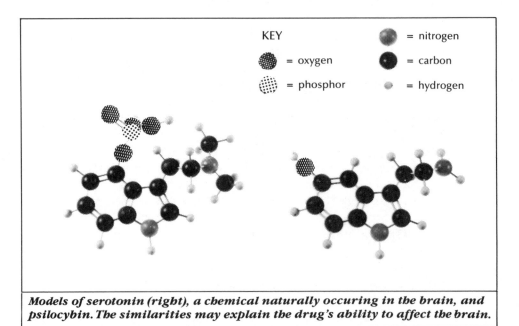

Models of serotonin (right), a chemical naturally occuring in the brain, and psilocybin. The similarities may explain the drug's ability to affect the brain.

many early users of this drug incorrectly felt the compound produced. DOM is a synthetic compound, first produced and reported in the chemical literature in 1964.

This literature provided "basement chemists" (people who use chemistry sets to produce drugs in their homes) with the necessary information to produce the drug. As a result, DOM became widely abused in the late 1960s. DOM is chemically related to the amphetamines (a group of drugs with similar chemical structures that stimulate the nervous system) and, therefore, produces some of the same effects: dilated pupils, rapid respiration, fast heartbeat, and increased blood pressure, in addition to its hallucinogenic effects.

Another LSD-like drug is psilocin, a synthetic drug closely related to the naturally occurring drug psilocybin. In fact, psilocybin is converted to psilocin within the body. Psilocybin is found in various species of mushrooms, including *Psilocybe mexicana*. There are some 15 species of this mushroom that grow wild in North America. This compound has also been used by the Aztec Indians in various religious ceremonies.

Another drug in this category is mescaline, which is found in the Peyote cactus and has long been used by

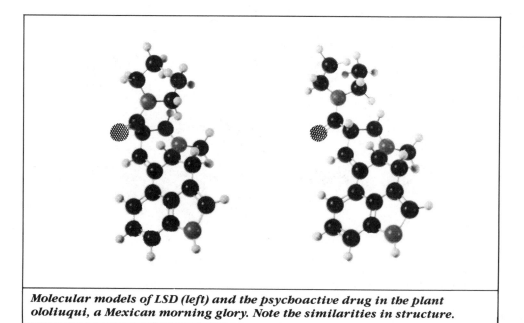

Molecular models of LSD (left) and the psychoactive drug in the plant ololiuqui, a Mexican morning glory. Note the similarities in structure.

American Indians in religious rituals. While all other LSD-like hallucinogens are strictly illegal drugs, the Native American Church has gotten permission from the United States Government to use mescaline in religious ceremonies and for medical purposes (such as a stimulant to respiration in patients with pneumonia and as a heart stimulant in patients with cardiovascular disease).

A fourth LSD-like drug is DMT, one of the many drugs that have been produced from plants such as *Mimosa, Virola,* and *Piptadenia.* These plants are used by South American Indians to prepare "hallucinogenic snuffs." Thus, in contrast to the other LSD-like hallucinogens, which are usually taken

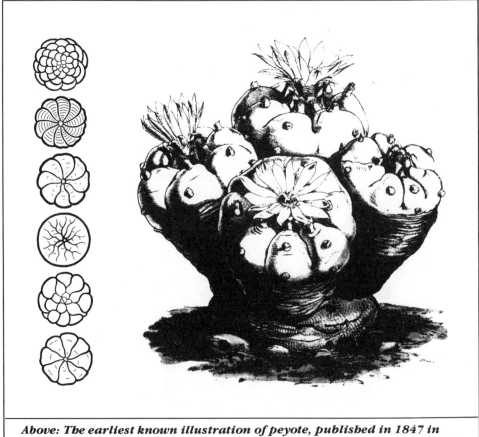

Above: The earliest known illustration of peyote, published in 1847 in Curtis' Botanical Magazine. *First described in 1560, it was not until 1845 that peyote was designated* Echinocactus williamsii. *Left: The crown of the peyote cactus takes on various forms, depending on its age.*

Summary of LSD and LSD-like Hallucinogens		
DRUG	SOURCE	LENGTH OF TIME USED BY MAN
lysergic acid diethylamide (LSD)	synthetic	Originally used in 1943; most popular from 1963 to 1967.
2,5-dimethoxy-4-methylamphetamine (DOM, STP)	synthetic	In use since 1964.
psilocin	*Psilocybe mexicana* mushroom	Used for centuries; psilocin isolated from the plant in 1958.
mescaline	peyote cactus	Used for centuries; mescaline isolated from the plant in 1896.
N,N-dimethyl-tryptamine (DMT)	*Mimosa, Virola* and *Piptadenia* plants	Used for centuries.

by mouth, DMT may be inhaled through the nostrils after the leaves have been dried and ground. DMT, however, is not nearly as potent an hallucinogen as the other LSD-like drugs.

Other Psychedelic Drugs

In addition to the above mentioned LSD-like drugs, there are other drugs sometimes classified as hallucinogens, psychedelics, or delusionogens that are different from LSD-like drugs. These are drugs that can produce true hallucinations in some individuals under certain circumstances, but usually produce quite different effects as their primary pharmacological activity (that is, the effects that the drug produces on the body). These drugs most frequently produce euphoria (an exaggerated sense of feeling good), relaxation, relief from anxiety, analgesia (relief of pain), stimulation, or some combination of these effects. These drugs include phencyclidine (PCP, angel dust), marijuana, various opiates (that is, narcotics such as morphine, heroin, and codeine), amphetamines, Valium, and scopolamine. While these drugs can, under certain circumstances, produce hallucinations, their overall pharmacological activity is very different from that of the LSD-like drugs. Therefore, these drugs will not be mentioned further here.

Street Names for LSD

acid	ghost	pure love
animal	grape parfait	purple barrels
barrels	green wedge	purple flats
beast	Hawaiian sunshine	purple haze
big D	hawk	purple hearts
black tabs	heavenly blue	purple ozoline
blotter	haze	royal blues
blue acid	instant zen	sacrament
blue chairs	"L"	Sandoz's
blue cheers	lason sa daga	smears
blue mist	LBJ	squirrel
blue vials	lids	strawberries
brown dots	Lucy in the sky with diamonds	strawberry fields
California sunshine	mellow yellows	sugar
cap	microdots	sugar lumps
chief	mighty Quinn	sunshine
chocolate chips	mind detergent	tabs
coffee	orange cubes	ticket
contact lens	orange micro	twenty-five
crackers	orange sunshine	vials
Cuba	orange wedges	wedding bells
cupcakes	Owsley	wedge
"D"	Owsley's blue dot	white lightning
Deeda	paper acid	white Owsley's
domes	peace	window pane
dot	peace tablets	yellow dimples
electric kool aid	pearly gates	yellows
flash	pellets	zen
flat blues	pink Owsley	
frogs	pink wedge	

It is important to be aware of the psychological, physiological, and behavioral effects of the LSD-like hallucinogens for several reasons. First, since these drugs are widely used, you should be able to recognize their symptoms should a friend or relative be using them and need help. Secondly, you should be aware of the toxicity (harmful effects) of these drugs before considering experimenting with them. Finally, you should be aware that LSD-like hallucinogens are frequently mixed with a wide variety of other drugs which, when combined, may cause death. Likewise, other drugs are frequently mixed with LSD to produce effects very different than expected. Since all of the LSD-like drugs and many of the other drugs of abuse are illegal and, therefore, purchased on the street, the buyer must put his trust in the seller. It is important to keep in mind that drug dealers are not known for their honesty.

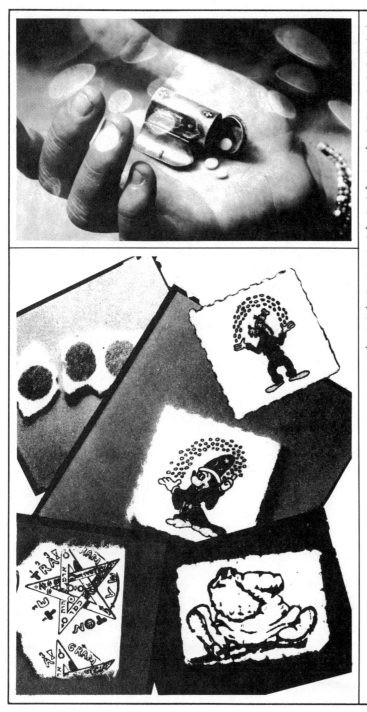

Habitual users of LSD and other hallucinogens created their own culture, colorfully embellished with new music, styles of dress, jewelry, and ornate paraphernalia. In the late 1970s blotter acid—paper previously soaked with LSD—became popular, and soon each dose was adorned with a cartoon character or symbol. Eventually each producer of LSD became associated with a particular, difficult to reproduce "label," and thus the user could be assured of the blotter's origin and content.

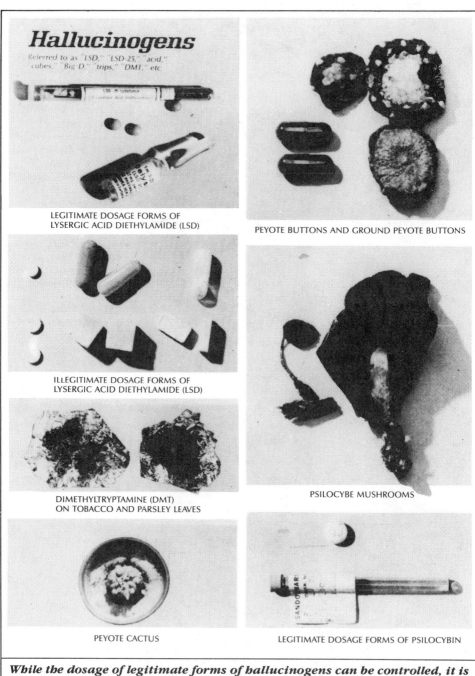

Hallucinogens

Referred to as "LSD," "LSD-25," "acid," cubes," "Big D," "trips," "DMT," etc.

LEGITIMATE DOSAGE FORMS OF
LYSERGIC ACID DIETHYLAMIDE (LSD)

PEYOTE BUTTONS AND GROUND PEYOTE BUTTONS

ILLEGITIMATE DOSAGE FORMS OF
LYSERGIC ACID DIETHYLAMIDE (LSD)

DIMETHYLTRYPTAMINE (DMT)
ON TOBACCO AND PARSLEY LEAVES

PSILOCYBE MUSHROOMS

PEYOTE CACTUS

LEGITIMATE DOSAGE FORMS OF PSILOCYBIN

While the dosage of legitimate forms of hallucinogens can be controlled, it is difficult to determine the dosage contained in organic or street forms.

Street Samples of LSD

Undercover agents have gone out onto the streets to buy LSD from drug dealers, and then turned the samples over to laboratory technicians for chemical analysis. One such study done in Canada revealed that 69% of the drugs sold as LSD were pure LSD, while 31% of the samples contained LSD plus some additional drug or no LSD whatsoever. This study also reported that LSD was found in samples sold as other drugs such as angel dust and barbiturates.

A similar study conducted in the United States in the early 1970s revealed that 82% of samples sold on the street as LSD were pure LSD, 3% were LSD-angel dust mixtures and 2% were pure angel dust. The remaining 13% of the samples were non-hallucinogenic compounds. This represents a deception rate of 18%. Other studies have found similar results and have uncovered the sale of LSD-amphetamine mixtures. This is a dangerous mixture since amphetamines grossly intensify the effects of LSD.

The deception rate for the sale of LSD on the street is relatively low in comparison with most other street drugs. For mescaline, only 1% of the street samples were pure mescaline. Sixty percent of these samples were pure LSD, 19% were LSD-angel dust mixtures, 4% were pure angel

Because drugs are illegal and relatively scarce, the drug user can become involved in many problems, including street crime and prostitution.

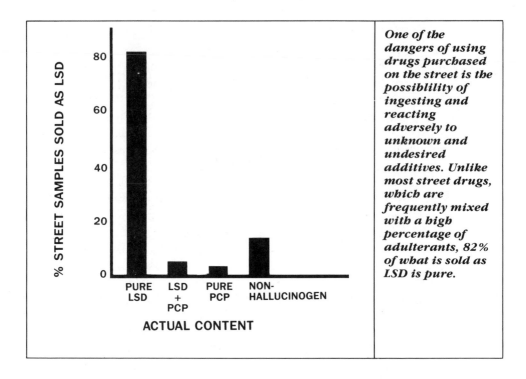

One of the dangers of using drugs purchased on the street is the possiblility of ingesting and reacting adversely to unknown and undesired additives. Unlike most street drugs, which are frequently mixed with a high percentage of adulterants, 82% of what is sold as LSD is pure.

dust, and 16% were a variety of non-hallucinogenic drugs. This represents a deception rate of 99% for street sales of mescaline.

The pattern is similar for psilocybin. Only 1% of the samples sold as psilocybin were pure drug, 68% were pure LSD, 9% were an LSD-angel dust mixture, 1% were pure angel dust, 1% were barbiturates, and 20% were a variety of other drugs. This represents a deception rate of 99%. From these studies we can see that many people who believe that they are buying some other hallucinogen on the street are actually receiving pure LSD or LSD mixed with some other drug. This probably reflects the relative ease of producing LSD in a pure form, as compared to the processes of obtaining some of these other drugs.

Another study found that only 49% of samples sold as amphetamine were pure drug, while 1% was angel dust, 1% was barbiturates, and 49% were numerous other drugs. This is a deception rate of 51%. For cocaine, 67% of samples were pure cocaine, 21% were cocaine-local anesthetic mixtures, 3% were pure local anesthetics, 2% were amphetamines, 1% was angel dust, and 6% were other drugs. For barbiturates, 59% were pure barbiturates, 3% were heroin, 2% were local anesthetics, 1% was amphetamine, and 35% were a variety of other drugs.

The only drug that was found to have a lower deception rate than LSD was marijuana, for which 90% of samples sold as marijuana contained the pure drug. Ten percent contained a variety of other drugs, with no marijuana present. This low deception rate is probably due to the fact that it is relatively easy to obtain marijuana in a pure form.

While this book will deal primarily with LSD, the other LSD-like drugs will be discussed when important similarities, differences, or drug interactions (that is, how one drug changes the effects of a second drug) deserve mention.

College students who use drugs fall into various categories: the curious who only try once; thrill seekers; those who surround their use of drugs with mysticism; those who are escaping reality; and those who are challenging authority. Pictured here is a marijuana cigarette resting on a sugar cube soaked with LSD.

"Now I'm opening out like the largest telescope that ever was! Good-bye feet!" cried Alice, in Alice in Wonderland. *Users of LSD often feel that they are either shrinking or stretching. When one woman unsuspectingly received 14 heavy doses of LSD over two months of psychotherapy, she had terrifying nightmares of feeling herself shrink like Alice, agonizing how she would get off her bed. Below, Alice, swimming in her own tears, passes a French-speaking mouse.*

CHAPTER 3

EFFECTS OF LSD

*M*any people take LSD and related hallucinogenic drugs because they feel that these drugs expand their consciousness and alter their moods. Some people, particularly writers, artists and musicians, also believe that LSD stimulates creativity. However, scientists studying artistic persons under the influence of LSD have concluded that creativity is clearly not enhanced by the drug. In fact, in many cases artistic ability was found to be diminished.

LSD is usually taken by mouth but may also be taken by injection, inhalation through the nose, or even by absorption through the skin. When taken by mouth, the individual usually notices the effects of the drug within 30 minutes. It may take approximately an hour before the user is "flying," that is, experiencing the maximal effects of the drug, and this state may last for 2-4 hours. The usual dose taken by mouth by the average-sized individual is approximately 50 to 100 micrograms, although much lower and higher doses have been used. The intensity of the hallucinatory experience is proportional to the dose taken. That is, low doses produce mild hallucinations, while high doses produce strong hallucinations. The psychological, perceptual and behavioral effects of LSD persist for 8 to 12 hours, and gradually wear off after reaching their maximal effects. They vary among individuals and vary within the same individual from episode to episode depending upon the social setting. There are variations among individuals in their response to LSD due solely to differing personality traits. The present chapter will be concerned with the psychological effects of LSD considered by the user to be good. The bad or toxic effects of LSD will be discussed in chapters 5 and 6.

Psychological Effects of LSD

Some of the effects most frequently reported by LSD users are feelings of depersonalization, a loss of body image, and derealization. This concept of depersonalization, while one of the most frequent effects of LSD, is one of the most difficult to describe. The individual's personality ("self" or "ego") seems to be divided into two parts: (a) an uninvolved observer and (b) a participating, involved self. The involved self is sometimes seen as an unidentified person that the user later recognizes as himself. The user is frequently unable to distinguish where his body ends and where the surrounding environment begins. The resulting behavior is not unlike that observed in infants who have not yet learned what parts belong to their body and what belongs to the surrounding environment. Derealization is a dream-like state in which the individual can not be sure whether he is experiencing reality or dreaming. This is a state that most people have experienced without having taken hallucinogenic drugs. It is comparable to the half-awake feeling following a dream when you are not certain whether you have just experienced a dream or reality.

Another common effect of LSD is alterations in perception of shape, size, color, and distance. A person under the

Photograph of a dime next to 1,000 micrograms of LSD (white dot). This seemingly innocent quantity of LSD would be sufficient to produce intense hallucinations in 10 to 20 normal individuals.

influence of LSD and related hallucinogens misjudges the size and distance of objects. The shapes of objects are also distorted and constantly changing. For example, one user of LSD reported that a cola bottle sitting in front of him suddenly appeared to melt and turn into an ashtray. Many times the objects change shape but not into anything recognizable. Fixed objects, such as furniture and walls, may appear to change in color and to move. In addition, objects that do not exist are seen and may also change in form and color. These objects can often be seen even when the LSD user closes his eyes since their image is produced within the mind. Also, colors frequently appear brighter and more intense than normal.

Another common effect of LSD is a phenomenon known as synesthesia, or a mixing of the senses. In synesthesia, experi-

Timothy Leary discusses LSD at the League for Spiritual Discovery, a religion he started in 1963. He hoped that it would show others how they could "help create every man as God and every woman as Goddess."

ences normally associated with one sense are translated into another. For example, sounds may be "seen," objects may be "heard," and colors may be "smelled." These changes are sometimes referred to as pseudo-hallucinations because the LSD user is usually capable of recognizing that these effects are drug-induced and usually remembers them clearly after the LSD episode is over.

Time is also often distorted by LSD with the user being unable to separate events from the past, present, and even

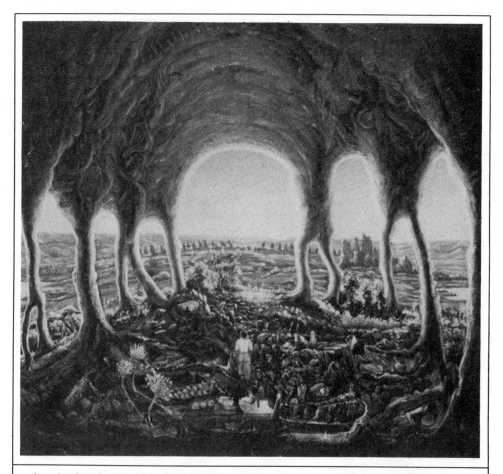

A painting by Yando, depicting an LSD experience. Many claim that LSD encourages creativity. In one instance architect Kyoshi Izoni, after taking LSD, visited and evaluated several conventionally designed mental institutions. His subsequent design for an "ideal mental hospital" was commended for outstanding architectural advancement.

future. A lack of concentration and gross impairment of judgement are also common. The user frequently experiences a profusion of vague ideas and may become preoccupied with ethical, moral, philosophical, or social issues, which he discusses freely with others. His descriptions of these issues are typically nonsensical to those not under the influence of the drug. An individual on LSD may remain completely motionless for long periods of time or may be hyperactive. The impairment of judgment may put the user, as well as those around him, in great danger since he may believe he can fly and jump off a building or feel that he can walk through walls or any number of other impossible acts. The LSD user will frequently ignore any type of life-threatening situation since he is convinced that his soul will live forever, making his body therefore insignificant. While relatively rare, a user of LSD will occasionally attack another person, apparently because he perceives that person as an enemy or evil force.

LSD can also produce rapid and dramatic changes in mood. An LSD user may feel great euphoria but not be able to explain why. A few minutes later he may feel extreme sadness and despair and, again, not be able to give a reason

During an LSD trip one often experiences distortions of time—one moment expanding until it seems to contain whole lifetimes. Allen Ginsberg, poet of the Beat Generation, compared it to a spirit investigating the "mysterious back alleys of the mind...going back into recollections of childhood...or forward into the future." Here White Rabbit has trouble with time.

for his feelings. There are no consistent effects of LSD on sexual behavior. Many have claimed that sex is more pleasurable under the influence of LSD, indicating that orgasms are more intense and prolonged. However, this is typically not the case. The LSD user's preoccupation with his own inner experience usually prevents any type of intimate activity with another person. The eroticism that occurs following LSD intake is largely mental, and the user is usually content to sit and concentrate on his hallucinatory experiences.

Another group of LSD-induced effects are referred to as "somatic symptoms." These include dizziness, weakness, tremors, blurred vision, and a creeping or tingling sensation of the skin. The skin sensations are probably tactile hallucinations. That is, the LSD user "feels" things on his skin when in fact nothing is there, just as he "sees" objects that do not exist.

Effects of LSD on the Body

In addition to the psychological effects of LSD described above, the drug also produces a number of physiological changes. LSD dilates the pupils of the eyes. It can also cause blurred vision and increases in the heart rate, blood pressure, and body temperature. The drug also increases blood sugar, produces alternating sweating and chills, and occasionally

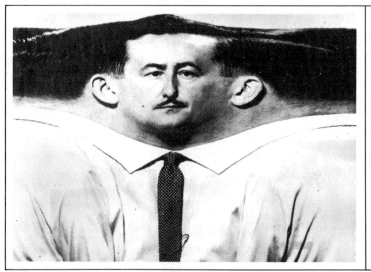

Though many have attempted to describe the LSD trip, ultimately the experience defies successful description. Even Henri Michaux, French poet and painter, stated that "it would require a picturesque style which I do not possess."

52

produces "goose pimples," headaches, dizziness, nausea, and vomiting. There are also changes in the muscles, resulting in weakness, tremors, numbness, and twitching. Abnormally rapid and deep breathing may also occur. These physiological effects, however, usually do not discourage the LSD user from continuing to use the drug.

Tolerance to LSD

Another important consideration with regard to the use of LSD is the phenomenon of tolerance. Tolerance is the capacity to adapt to the drug. As tolerance increases, the psychological and physiological effects become less dramatic with

St. Anthony, patron saint of ergotism victims. In the Middle Ages the fungus ergot was sometimes inadvertently baked into bread. Those who ate it experienced what was called "St. Anthony's fire." Sometimes hands and feet blackened and fell off. Thousands died.

Psychological Effects of LSD

PERCEPTUAL EFFECTS
  Heightened sensory experience
  Colors appear more intense than normal
  Visual hallucinations; "seeing" objects that do not exist
  Visual distortion of objects present in the environment
  Distortion of time sense
  Synesthesia, or a mixing of senses; i.e., one hears color or sees music
  Distortion of distance judgment and impaired coordination
  Distortion of body image
  Distortion of space
  Derealization, or a dream-like feeling
  Creeping or tingling sensation of the skin
  Depersonalization; boundaries between self and environment disappear

INTELLECTUAL EFFECTS
  Gross impairment of judgment
  Inability to concentrate
  Surfacing of memories
  Inability to control thoughts
  Fixation on trivial ideas
  False belief that one possesses profound philosophical insight

MOOD EFFECTS
  Rapid and dramatic mood changes (euphoria-depression)
  Hyperactivity, inactivity, or alteration between these two states
  Simultaneous existence of different emotions
  A profound mystical or religious experience

Physiological Effects of LSD

MUSCULAR EFFECTS	Weakness Twitching Tremors
NEUROLOGICAL EFFECTS	Numbness Dizziness Headache Blurred vision Dilation of pupils
CARDIOVASCULAR EFFECTS	Increased heart rate Increased blood pressure
GASTROINTESTINAL EFFECTS	Nausea Vomiting Appetite suppression Increaed sugar metabolism
BODY TEMPERATURE EFFECTS	Increased body temperature Sweating Chills
RESPIRATORY EFFECTS	Increased respiration rate Deep breathing

each consecutive dose. Tolerance develops to LSD very rapidly. In most individuals a single dose of the drug will produce some tolerance. That is, if a person takes 100 micrograms of LSD one day and experiences a certain degree of hallucinatory activity and then takes a second dose of 100 micrograms the next day, he will not experience as prominent an hallucinatory effect on the second day. If a person takes 100 micrograms of LSD each day for four or five consecutive days, he will usually experience no hallucinations at all by the fifth day. As tolerance develops, the user has to take a much higher dose of the drug (say, 500 or 1000 micrograms) in order to produce an hallucinatory episode. If the person goes for a few days without the drug, the tolerance will disappear and he will again be able to

In Alice in Wonderland *the executioner wondered how one could "cut off a head unless there is a body to cut it off from," while the King stated that "anything that had a head could be beheaded." On LSD, a person may discover a world that has slipped the chains of normal ordering, and a consciousness which is multiple or fragmented. Often there is an exaggerated concern with philosophical and religious questions.*

experience an intense hallucinatory episode with 100 micrograms or so of the drug. Thus, the tolerance disappears as quickly as it develops, assuming the individual does not take any LSD during the interim.

In contrast to many other psychoactive drugs, LSD is rarely used every day. This is partly due to the tolerance that develops. Many regular users of LSD are "weekend trippers," using the drug for recreational purposes on weekends and vacation days only. Many others will try LSD once or twice out of pure curiosity about the drug's effects and then never use it again.

Effects of Other Hallucinogens

The other LSD-like drugs (DOM, mescaline, psilocin, and DMT) produce psychic and physiological effects very similar to those produced by LSD. Each drug produces some unique effects but on the whole all result in similar hallucinatory experiences. There is, however, quite a large difference in the potency of the various drugs. Potency refers to the amount of the drug that must be given to produce a given effect. LSD, as mentioned earlier, is the most potent hallucinatory drug. DOM is the next most potent, followed by psilocin, mescaline, and DMT.

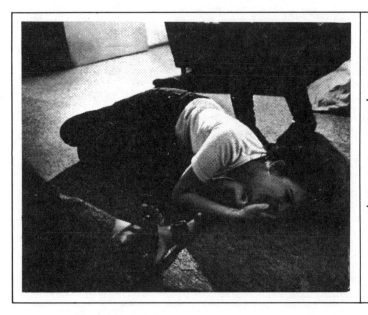

A "bummer" can be productive if the user is guided through it and allowed to learn from the negative experience. Here, a teenager writhes on the floor, horrified by visions of self-mutilation. Later she returned home for the first time in a year.

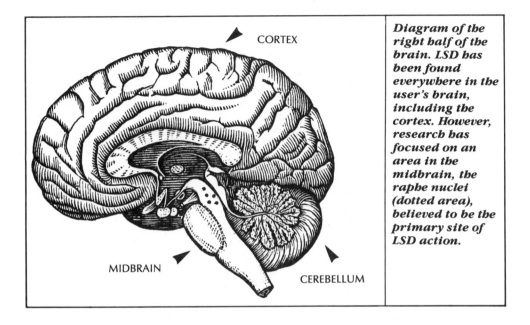

CORTEX

MIDBRAIN

CEREBELLUM

Diagram of the right half of the brain. LSD has been found everywhere in the user's brain, including the cortex. However, research has focused on an area in the midbrain, the raphe nuclei (dotted area), believed to be the primary site of LSD action.

How LSD Works

Despite the fact that LSD and related hallucinogens have been under scientific study for approximately 25 years, their mechanism of action is not fully known. That is, we do not yet know how LSD produces its characteristic psychological effects. It has been shown that LSD binds to specific receptor sites in the brain and that these receptor sites are widely distributed throughout the brain. However, the manner in which LSD produces its psychological effects after binding to these sites has not been determined. This is currently an active area of research, and an answer to the question of how LSD and related drugs can produce such dramatic psychological effects in such small doses will hopefully soon be answered. It is worth noting that LSD shows cross-tolerance with other drugs in this class. That is, if an individual takes several doses of LSD and becomes tolerant to the psychological effects of LSD, he will also be tolerant to the usual doses of DOM, psilocin, DMT, and mescaline. This suggests that all of the drugs may have a similar mechanism of action in the brain, and if that mechanism is discovered for one drug, the mechanism will be known for all of the drugs in this class.

The Haight-Ashbury community was characterized by the widespread use of LSD and other drugs. As opposed to the beatniks who focused on the individual and wore black and white clothes, members of this new community wore bright, multicolored clothes and believed in communal living. Life here was energized by the music of such groups as the Jefferson Airplane and the Grateful Dead, by psychedelic artwork, and supported by the Free Clinic and the Diggers, who gave away food and clothing.

CHAPTER 4

THE LSD EXPERIENCE

*L*SD is now a recreational drug. Recreational drugs are those that have nonmedical uses or are used for nonmedical purposes. Most recreational drugs are used in social settings. Just as most people use alcohol in social settings, most LSD users practice their drug habit with their peers as well. Thus, LSD would generally be classified as a social drug, one which brings people together. Furthermore, it tends to attract people with similar interests and backgrounds. Social drug usage creates an atmosphere in which people are more likely to share experiences and feelings than they otherwise would. With LSD and related hallucinogens, as in the case of certain other drugs, the type of social setting can dramatically influence the behavioral and psychological effects of the drug. On the other hand, use of LSD or other hallucinogens can dramatically alter one's social interactions. Therefore, we have a situation in which there is a complex interrelationship between the effects of the drug on the individual, and the effects of the social environment on the individual.

First of all, it is worth pointing out that LSD was used most commonly in the 1960s in social groups. Dr. Leary originally held sessions in which numerous people got together to take LSD and then share their innermost feelings. The practice spread. Soon users of LSD developed their own jargon, which was an intimate part of the social environment in which the drugs were taken. For example, LSD is commonly referred to as "acid." A person who uses LSD frequently is called an "acid head." The hallucinatory experience is called a "trip," and the person experiencing a "bad trip" is "freaking out." If a person is an experienced LSD user, he is called a "guru." One who goes along on a "trip" is a "co-pilot." The person who supplies the LSD is a "travel agent." If a person adds LSD to the punch bowl at a social gathering, the party is called an "acid test." Finally, a person who stops a friend from jumping off a building is "ground control." All of this colorful terminology grew from social situations where people gathered to take LSD.

The response of a given individual to LSD at a given time depends upon the personality of the individual, his previous drug history, existing medical conditions, the social environment in which the drug is taken, and the dosage. At this point, we should emphasize that the effects of personality traits and social environment are frequently difficult to separate. That is, it is very difficult to say that a particular effect is due to the personality of the individual and another effect is attributable to the social environment, since the two factors are closely linked. More specifically, the personality of the individual determines, at least in part, the nature of his social interactions. Because of so many variables, it is

In 1967 the Beatles, in their record "Sergeant Pepper's Lonely Hearts Club Band," sang about LSD and the search within, claiming that "we're all one, and life flows on within you and without you." Three years earlier they had told the 1960s generation to "Turn off your mind, relax, and float downstream/This is not dying."

During the 1960s music enthusiast Bill Graham presented the most popular rock groups at the Fillmore West in San Francisco. Bands such as Creedence Clearwater Revival and Santana played to wildly attired audiences which packed the house. Disillusioned by the advent of high-priced superstars, Graham finally backed out of the era of rock music on July 14, 1966, when he staged the final performance at the Fillmore.

August 1969: an estimated 300,000 rock music fans congregated at a former cow pasture for the Woodstock Music and Art Festival. Drugs abounded. The festival did feature some of the best music of the period, from such groups as Santana; Crosby, Stills, Nash and Young; and Joni Mitchell.

Woodstock represented a cross section of the 1960s generation, expressing everything from wild enthusiasm to extreme desperation.

difficult to predict how a given individual will react to LSD. We can, however, make some important generalizations.

Expectation and Social Setting

If an individual has never taken LSD before, his expectations will play an important role in what he actually experiences under the influence of the drug. There is a large element of suggestibility in the use of LSD and related hallucinogens. If his friends have taken the drug and tell him what to expect, he may well experience effects very similar to theirs. If the person has had previous experience with LSD, he anticipates, sometimes wrongly, a hallucinatory experience based on earlier "trips." Reactions also depend upon mood at the time the drug is taken and motivation for taking the drug. Motivation, in fact, is always a factor in the resulting hallucinatory experience. If the person takes LSD because he wants to have a "mind-expanding" or "consciousness-raising" experience, he is more likely to have a good trip. On the other hand, if he is taking the drug because of peer pressure, that is, because most of his friends are taking the drug and he does not wish to be considered different or unusual, he is much more likely to have a bad trip, or "bummer" as it is frequently called. In fact, when an individual has a lot of anxiety about taking the drug, he usually has a bad trip.

In general, then, an individual is more likely to have a good trip on LSD if he has had previous good experiences with the drug, is motivated to take the drug for the purposes

When in 1967 President Johnson passed a bill which made LSD illegal, drug use had already been linked with anti-establishment activities. As the number of protests grew so did confrontations with authorities.

of "expanding his mind" or "raising his consciousness," and takes the drug in the presence of good friends who are supportive of his actions, even though they may not themselves be taking the drug. It is important to point out that, despite what the user may think, there is no evidence that LSD or other hallucinogens "expand the mind," "raise consciousness," or increase creativity. It is the user's attitudes towards the drug, not the actual facts, which influence the hallucinatory experience.

Personality Traits and Past Drug Experience

In general, LSD tends to intensify the user's natural personality traits. If a person is very out-going to begin with, he may become even more so under the influence of the drug. He may become hyperactive and overly talkative, passing from one individual to the next to share his hallucinatory experience. If he is a more introverted or quiet type of individual, he may simply sit quietly in some out-of-the-way place and concentrate on his own feelings while going through the hallucinatory experience.

This is not always the case, however. LSD may turn a very sociable person into one who is antisocial. By contrast, a person who is naturally quiet may become much more sociable under the influence of LSD.

In summary, it is difficult to predict how a given individual will react to LSD since the psychological effects of the

In a symbolic gesture, hippies burn dollar bills outside the New York Stock exchange. During the peak of the alternative culture, many who believed in the established system, which stressed money, power, and status, were threatened by the hippies, who strove to change people's goals and values.

drug are dependent upon so many factors. We can conclude, however, that the most important factors are: social environment, the personality of the user, his previous experience with the drug, his expectations, his motivation for taking the drug, his attitude toward the use of such drugs, and the individuals with whom he interacts while under the influence of LSD.

The effects of LSD on the individual and on his social interactions are quite different from those of marijuana, heroin, cocaine, amphetamine, alcohol, and sedative-hypnotics, such as Valium. These drugs produce euphoria and may tend to enhance social interactions. LSD, on the other hand, does not produce euphoria to any great extent. When it does, it is usually short-lived and not as strong as that produced by marijuana, heroin, or even alcohol. The hallucinations that follow LSD intake mask or cover up the euphoric effect of the drug. Furthermore, with certain drugs, such as marijuana and alcohol, use of the drug is an integral part of the social interaction. That is, passing around a "joint" at a "pot party" or drinks at a cocktail party is an important part of the overall social ritual. This is not so with LSD. An individual takes one dose of LSD and its effects last for 8 to 12 hours. There is no passing the drug around. Thus, there is an inherent difference in the social interactions that accompany the use of the different types of drugs.

As the popularity of LSD spread there was also a burst of creativity. Both artists and nonartists experimented with brilliant, glowing colors and flowing lines, embellishing everything including murals, cars, canvases and faces.

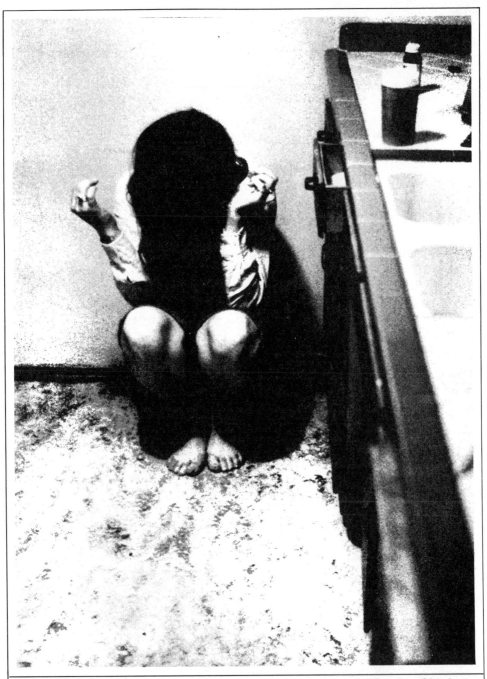

As LSD takes effect, the user may begin to plunge into the depths of both the conscious and unconscious self. Along the way the body may be perceived as a tool, a vehicle, a plaything, an encumbrance, a source of pain and pleasure, a source of wonder, or the "temple of the spirit."

CHAPTER 5

FLASHBACKS

One of the most puzzling and dangerous aspects of LSD usage is the phenomenon of the flashback. Flashbacks occur primarily after the use of LSD but may occur after the use of related hallucinogens as well. They do not appear to occur following the use of any type of psychoactive drug other than the hallucinogens.

What Is a Flashback?

A flashback is defined as a transitory, spontaneous recurrence of certain aspects of the LSD hallucinatory experience after a period of normal brain functioning following the original ingestion of LSD. Flashbacks first became widely publicized in 1970 when the daughter of television personality Art Linkletter committed suicide during a flashback about six months after she had taken LSD. Since that time the flashback has been extensively studied but its cause still remains a mystery. Scientists have, however, learned several important facts about the phenomenon.

When Do Flashbacks Occur?

A flashback may occur after a single dose of LSD but usually occurs in people who use the drug chronically. When a flashback occurs after only one exposure to LSD, the original trip was usually a bad one. A single good trip rarely results in the occurrence of flashbacks. Although flashbacks occur more frequently in people that have some underlying personality problem, they can occur in a normal individual. Flashbacks typically have all the qualities of the original LSD experience. The individual experiences the psychic effects, hallucinations, mood swings, depersonalization, and derealization. Flashbacks may occur within a few days after LSD use or a few weeks, months, or even years. They may last a few minutes or for several hours. They may occur several times a day, once a week, once a month, or just one time.

Although flashbacks may occur at any time, there are certain times in which they are more likely to occur, such as during times of stress. They also occur frequently just before the individual goes to sleep or while he is driving a car, which is particularly dangerous. Flashbacks also frequently occur when the individual is intoxicated with another type of psychoactive drug, such as alcohol, tranquilizers, amphet-

Television personality Art Linkletter with two of his daughters in 1957. Thirteen years later Diane, the youngest daughter, was to fall to her death while experiencing severe and disturbing LSD flashbacks.

amines, or marijuana. In addition, flashbacks can be triggered by the company of another person under the influence of LSD or by bright flashing lights such as might occur at a rock concert. It is important to know, however, that a flashback may occur at any time with no obvious triggering event.

Types of Flashbacks

Flashbacks have been categorized into three types: emotional, somatic, and perceptual. Of the three, the emotional flashback is the most dangerous. It brings back powerful feelings of panic, fear, and loneliness similar to those experienced during a bad trip. The person will frequently attempt suicide under these circumstances. A somatic flashback consists of altered bodily sensations similar to those experienced dur-

After his daughter's death, Art Linkletter began a personal crusade to provide information about drugs and drug abuse. Though he favored lenient penalties for first-time marijuana users, he became an advisor to President Nixon, with whom he often disagreed. Linkletter claimed that the president tended to simplify the drug issue, seeing it as black and white rather than a blend of grays.

ing a bad LSD trip. These include tremors, weakness, nausea, dizziness, and a creeping or tingling sensation of the skin. Somatic flashbacks almost always occur after a bad LSD trip. The individual is frequently frightened and has a lot of anxiety because of this condition but usually does not try to commit suicide. The third and most common type of flashback is the perceptual flashback, in which the individual experiences the perceptual distortions of vision, hearing, smell, taste, and touch that characterized the original LSD trip. This type of flashback is usually not dangerous to the individual (unless he is driving a car), and in some cases the individual actually enjoys the episode.

While flashbacks have received much attention from scientists and physicians, the brain mechanisms which produce them are still not known. It was originally believed that LSD remained in the body for very long periods of time, and the flashback was a manifestation of the sudden release of LSD stored somewhere in the body. However, it was later determined that all LSD is gone from the body within approximately 24 hours, so the stored-LSD hypothesis was abandoned.

It is generally accepted that LSD produces long-term or permanent changes within the brain. Interestingly, this may occur following a single dose of the drug, as described earlier. Therefore, it is possible that a person's brain will never be the same after taking even a single dose of LSD. Hopefully, future research in this area will identify the changes that occur in the brain and produce a method for reversing them. It will probably take many years, however.

In the meantime there are certain measures that should be taken in dealing with a person who is experiencing flashbacks. Since they are frequently triggered by other psychoactive drugs, the former LSD user would be wise never to take any other drugs. They should also avoid the other factors that can trigger a flashback: stress, bright flashing lights, and crowded places. Psychotherapy can also help to relieve anxiety about the condition. In some cases, sedatives such as Valium or phenobarbital have been used to control this anxiety, but they have not been successful in controlling the occurrence of flashbacks. In the case of flashbacks that occur just before sleep, potent sleep-inducing drugs have been shown in many cases to stop the flashbacks.

Since flashbacks occur most frequently following a bad LSD trip, it is possible to prevent them in some cases by turning a bad trip into a good one. This can often be done by a trusted and reassuring friend.

In conclusion, it should be obvious that LSD can be a very dangerous drug. Indeed, some people have died from using it, not from an overdose but as a result of their actions during the hallucinatory experience. LSD is not an addicting drug, such as heroin, but it can be habit forming, and the effects of chronic LSD usage can be very serious. Most importantly, once a person has taken LSD, even a single dose, he may suffer from recurrent flashbacks for months or years, even though he never takes the drug again. Thus, this seems to be much too great a risk to take for a few hours of a (possibly) enjoyable hallucinatory experience.

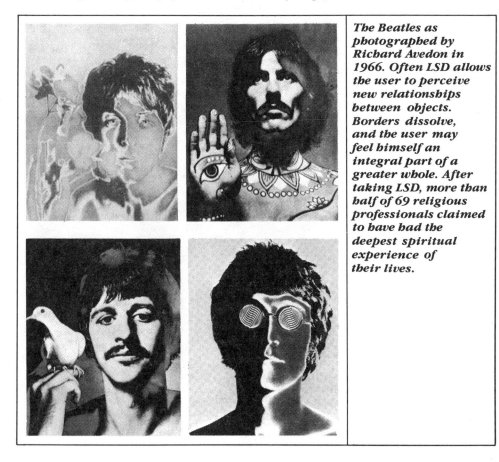

The Beatles as photographed by Richard Avedon in 1966. Often LSD allows the user to perceive new relationships between objects. Borders dissolve, and the user may feel himself an integral part of a greater whole. After taking LSD, more than half of 69 religious professionals claimed to have had the deepest spiritual experience of their lives.

LSD can take you places you never dreamt of.

This poster of a youth straitjacketed and in a padded cell was distributed by a British social work organization. Though the alterations of consciousness produced by LSD can lead to impairment, in fact this is extremely rare. Circumstances, dosage, drug quality, and companionship all affect the quality of the LSD experience.

CHAPTER 6

TOXIC EFFECTS OF LSD

LSD is capable of producing toxic effects, some of which are relatively mild and others which are very severe. They can be divided into two categories, acute and chronic. Acute toxic effects are those that occur after a single or very few doses of the drug. The effects of chronic toxicity are those that occur after the individual has taken LSD repeatedly over a long period of time.

The "Bad Trip"

The mildest and most common type of acute LSD toxicity is the "bad trip," or "bummer" as it is frequently called. The bummer usually happens as follows. Shortly after taking the drug, the user feels that he has "lost it," meaning that he does not feel that he has control over his thoughts, perceptions, and behavior and wants out immediately. This usually leads to panic, followed by confusion and, in some cases, psychological depression. The person might even attempt to jump out of a window or rush wildly down a busy street to escape the bad trip. The bummer occurs most frequently in people who have never taken the drug before and are frightened by the hallucinatory experience. They may think that spiders are crawling all over their body or feel that they are about to fall into a bottomless pit. Individuals with psychiatric problems are also much more likely to have a bummer than well-adjusted persons.

It is often difficult to tell whether a bummer is caused by LSD alone or whether it is caused by LSD contaminated with some other psychoactive drug. Since LSD is an illegal drug it must be purchased on the street. Drug dealers will frequently mix various psychoactive drugs and sell them as a pure form of one of the drugs. For example, it has been learned that amphetamines are frequently added to LSD. The amphetamine, a strong stimulant, increases the effects of LSD.

Careful laboratory studies have shown, however, that LSD alone can result in a bad trip. Yet there is no way to predict which persons will have an adverse reaction to LSD.

New Year's Eve at the Fillmore. When at midnight a loincloth-clad figure rode on a white horse through the crowd and released white doves, the audience roared.

During the 1960s the hippie movement focused on changing life styles and challenging traditional values. Here, in a forest near Boulder, Colorado, one hippie sits in front of his plastic tent, surrounded by his belongings.

There is also no explanation as to why a person will have an adverse reaction on one occasion but not another. It is known that a person may have a bad trip even after more than 100 trips without any bummers.

LSD and Psychotic Reactions

A more serious toxic effect of LSD is a psychotic reaction. In fact, LSD is sometimes considered a "psychotomimetic," that is, a drug that elicits psychotic states similar to schizophrenia. A paranoid reaction frequently occurs in which the individual believes that everyone is "out to get him." He feels that he cannot trust anyone. He may even feel that others, even his friends, are plotting to kill him. During LSD-induced psychotic states, people frequently suffer from what psychiatrists call "delusions of grandeur." This means that the person actually believes that he is superhuman, able to do things that are obviously impossible. For example, people under the influence of LSD sometimes believe that they can fly and will jump out of windows or off roofs. Others imagine that they are some famous person or important historical figure. Some people under the influence of LSD believe that they are Jesus Christ. Others, thinking themselves indestructible, shoot themselves with a gun, stab themselves, or try to run through walls. Thus, several accidental suicides occur each year due to LSD-induced psychotic states. In addition, some people purposely commit suicide while under the influence of LSD because the drug produces such a severe psychological depression in these individuals that they do not want to live.

The paranoid reactions described earlier have also led certain people to attempt murder. A person may become so suspicious of other people, even his closest friends, that he believes they are plotting against him. The user may therefore attempt to murder his friends. In his mind, the paranoid user believes he is acting in self-defense, since he is thoroughly convinced that others are planning to harm him. While no accurate statistics on murders or attempted murders by users of LSD are available, this is apparently a rare occurrence. The LSD-precipitated psychosis ordinarily lasts for a few hours. However, sometimes the psychosis lasts much longer.

A single dose of LSD can precipitate a psychosis that lasts for approximately one month, although it usually lasts a few hours. This long-term reaction to the drug is relatively rare and the reason for the effect is not known. The most common type of long-term effect following a single dose of LSD is a schizophrenic state. This is most often the paranoid type, that is, when an individual is suspicious of everything that other people do and misinterprets things that they say. Other types of persisting toxic reactions that may follow a single dose of LSD are depression, mania (hyperactivity), and a catatonic state in which the individual will sit, stand, or lie in a certain position for several hours at a time without moving. In some cases, these toxic reactions go away, only to reappear a few weeks later despite no drug use during the interim. It is possible that people who experi-

In 1969 at the Altamont Speedway near Livermore, California, a rock concert attended by 300,000 enthusiasts and policed by Hell's Angels ended with violence, injuries, and deaths. Many in the audience had ingested adulterated LSD, in addition to heroin, amphetamines, barbiturates, and alcohol. Some labeled this the end of the dream which began in 1965 on Haight Street.

ence these reactions are borderline psychotics to begin with, and the drug merely precipitates psychotic behavior. Approximately 40% of the cases of prolonged psychoses are known to have occurred following the first dose of LSD. This supports the idea that these people may have been psychotic to begin with, since LSD is more likely to produce psychoses in a normal individual only after repeated use.

LSD and Convulsions

Another severe toxic effect of LSD is convulsions, although these are rare. There have been only seven cases of grand mal (major) seizures due to LSD use reported in the medical literature. However, people are often reluctant to admit habits and effects of illegal drugs, so there may be a considerably higher incidence of LSD-induced convulsions than we are aware of. Current evidence, however, indicates that convulsions are a rare but definite effect of LSD usage.

The Effects of an Overdose

It is not known with certainty whether any deaths have been due to LSD overdose (that is, independent of suicides or accidental deaths). Humans have been known to take up to 2000-3000 micrograms of LSD (40 to 60 times the usual dose for a potent hallucinatory experience) and have survived with no apparent ill effects. From studies done with animals, it can be estimated that it would take approximately 15,000 micrograms to kill a human being. Since this

LSD pioneer Walter Clark claimed that LSD "adds nothing to our consciousness, but it brings to the surface many parts of our consciousness that had been lying dormant most of our lives. The typical person . . . turns out to be a mystic."

dose is so far above that needed to produce an intense hallucinatory episode, it is unlikely that anyone would ever take nearly enough LSD to cause death.

Effects of Repeated Use of LSD

Three notable behavioral syndromes may occur as the result of LSD use over an extended period of time. The first is the "amotivational syndrome." (This pattern has also been observed in chronic users of marijuana.) As the name implies, this syndrome is characterized by a lack of motivation. In many cases the individual becomes so incapacitated by the amotivational syndrome that he is unable to function in society. The individual loses interest in work, school, hobbies— all the things that he derived satisfaction from prior to his long-term involvement with LSD. He is incapable of making long-range plans and lives solely for the present. He becomes lazy and ineffective in nearly everything he tries to do, and is easily frustrated. The person often becomes preoccupied with the drug and looks forward to nothing but taking LSD.

A second toxic effect of prolonged LSD use is generally referred to as the "psychedelic syndrome." This syndrome is characterized by an interest in astrology, extrasensory perception, mental telepathy, mysticism, and magic. Long-time LSD users often become so preoccupied with these

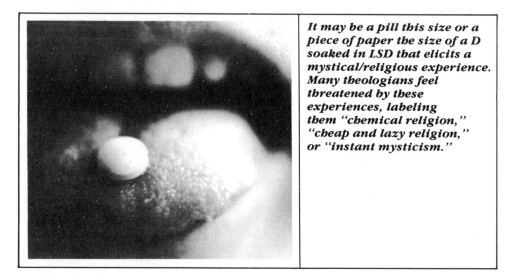

It may be a pill this size or a piece of paper the size of a D soaked in LSD that elicits a mystical/religious experience. Many theologians feel threatened by these experiences, labeling them "chemical religion," "cheap and lazy religion," or "instant mysticism."

phenomena that they devote their full attention to them and, in effect, drop out of normal society.

A third toxic effect of LSD use is a persistent anxiety. In this condition, the person is always anxious and frequently experiences physiological symptoms and mental depression.

It is important to point out that the above syndromes do not always follow chronic LSD use. Many people have taken LSD frequently over several years without any noticeable toxic effects. However, it is clear that all of the above are possible consequences.

Another possible effect of chronic LSD use is irreversible changes in the brain. Occasionally, studies have shown that the electroencephalogram (brain wave patterns) appears abnormal in some individuals who have taken LSD frequently over a period of years. It is not known, however, whether

In a symbolic gesture to emphasize the influence of the Beatles and their music on both the drug culture and anti-establishment behavior, Jeremy Lyle, a born-again Christian from California, destroys $2,000 worth of rare records. Those who were involved in the activities of the 1960s often claim that the post-1960s generation is reactionary and readily accepts those values the preceding generation fought to change.

the individuals tested would have shown abnormal brain wave patterns without taking LSD.

As mentioned earlier, reports that LSD damaged chromosomes was one of the reasons that the drug became less popular during the late 1960s. These early studies examined the effects of very high concentrations of LSD on chromosomes in test tubes. Although the doses used in these studies were higher than any person would ever take, recent tests have provided new evidence that LSD can indeed cause damage to chromosomes. It is important to note, however, that drug users seldom take only one drug. Therefore there are extremely few, if any, people who use only LSD. Most individuals use other drugs, such as marijuana and amphetamines, in addition to LSD. Therefore, it is difficult to determine whether the chromosomal damage that has been noted is due to LSD, some other psychoactive drug, or to a combination of LSD and other drugs.

The effects of LSD toxicity on fertility, pregnancy, and birth defects are also being studied. While there are no highly accurate statistical data available on this topic, clinical impressions and fragments of data are available and should be mentioned. First of all, pregnancy is less frequent

Psychedelic art, which grew out of the use of LSD and other hallucinogens, frequently focused on repetitive lines and shapes. Often, as here, the artwork took on the form of mandalas, graphic symbols often used by Eastern mystics to aid deep meditation.

among users of LSD than among the general population. There also appears to be a very high rate of spontaneous abortions among LSD users. This may be due to certain pharmacological actions of the drug. That is, the drug may act to alter uterine contractions, fetal blood flow, or other factors that could result in abortion. Another important consideration is that chronic LSD users are frequently undernourished and vulnerable to many infectious diseases. Therefore, it could be a combination of malnourishment, diseases, and other drugs, together with LSD use, that results in this high rate of spontaneous abortion.

Data concerning birth defects are also scanty. However, there is some evidence that the use of LSD during pregnancy can be harmful to the child. One study examined dead fetuses and infants who died shortly after birth and whose mothers were all LSD users. The incidence of brain defects was 16 times higher than in the general population.

Toxic Effects of LSD

Acute Toxicity

1. "Bad trip"—leading to panic, severe confusion, depression, loss of identity, and hallucinations
2. Paranoid psychotic reactions
3. Convulsions
4. Psychological depression which persists for a few days following a single drug dose
5. Mania
6. Hyperexcitability
7. Catatonia
8. Violent homicidal or suicidal tendencies

Chronic Toxicity

1. Amotivational syndrome
2. Psychedelic syndrome
3. Persistent anxiety
4. Possible irreversible changes in brain wave pattern
5. Possible chromosomal damage
6. Impaired fertility
7. Flashbacks

Some researchers and therapists have chosen biofeedback as a substitute for and a way to combat drug abuse. According to Dr. Jeff Nichols, a psychotherapist, biofeedback "machines are tools we use to help the person gain increased awareness. [They help] people cultivate positive images of themselves."

CHAPTER 7

THERAPY FOR ABUSERS OF LSD

Why would anyone want to risk taking a drug as toxic as LSD? The reasons are many and varied. Some people take it to enjoy the hallucinatory experience. This, in fact, is the most common reason for taking the drug. Others take the drug to escape reality. Another reason for taking LSD is peer pressure. Whatever the reasons, it is important to know what treatments are available to individuals experiencing acute and chronic LSD toxicity. In most cases, it is important that the chronic LSD user stop taking drugs because eventually he is likely to harm himself or another person.

Persons experiencing bad LSD trips who are taken to hospital emergency rooms are usually given a drug called a neuroleptic. These are the same drugs usually given to schizophrenic patients to help control their disordered thought processes and behavioral abnormalities. While a neuroleptic drug decreases the intensity of the hallucinations, they still continue for some time but at a much milder level. In addition to drug therapy, other supportive measures are taken. The individual is kept under surveillance to ensure that he does not attempt to harm himself or others. He is kept in a calm and pleasant environment. It also helps to have a good friend present to talk to the user to reassure him that he will be all right. After a few hours the effects of the drug usually wear off completely and the individual is free to go home.

Unfortunately, there is no good drug treatment for a chronic LSD user. Furthermore, there is no way to identify a chronic LSD user if he is not on a trip at the time of observation. Nor are there any strong physiological signs associated with LSD use. Even a detailed examination by a physician probably would not uncover chronic LSD use.

Psychotherapy

The key to stopping a dangerous LSD habit is to remove the reason for taking the drug and to substitute some other form of activity. Education plays an important role in this process. The individual must come to understand that the drug is a very toxic one and that continued use may well lead to very serious health problems. However, education alone is usually not sufficient. Psychotherapy is often needed. Various

During the 1960s the Haight-Ashbury Free Clinic was open around the clock and served anyone needing help. One room was set aside specifically for those who had taken an hallucinogen and required assistance.

psychoanalytic theories assume that a patient with a psychiatric problem has undergone a general regression to child-like thinking. It is further assumed that the patient experiences the emergence of repressed memories and other information. Many investigators have suggested that LSD, especially when taken chronically, also releases suppressed memories and other information that is unpleasant to the patient. Therefore, the LSD abuser must learn to deal with these child-like patterns of thought. During psychotherapy the LSD abuser undergoes an emotional re-education.

The goals of therapy are to acquire more positive feelings about one's self and to learn to solve problems in a constructive, creative, and mature way. Negative feelings and self-defeating behavior are dealt with during psychotherapy. If the individual has taken LSD solely for a good trip (the most common reason for taking the drug), he must find a new activity to substitute for his drug habit. This is easier said than done. Individuals who have experienced good

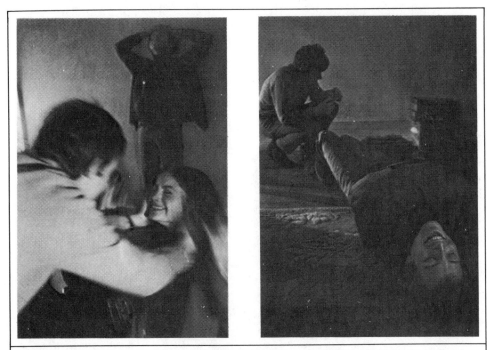

While often it is peer pressure which pushes a person to first experiment with LSD, peer support is important when combatting a bad trip or when fighting the lure of another LSD experience.

trips often have a strong drive to continue them. Persons who take LSD chronically to escape reality because they are unhappy need to take positive steps to improve their lives. Taking drugs to escape from life is a cop out. One must learn to deal with the stresses and disappointments that are common to living. The problem will still be there when the trip, no matter how good, is over.

Learning to Cope with Peer Pressure

Individuals who take LSD due to peer pressure must learn to have the courage to say no. A person must learn to think for himself and not let his actions be determined by others around him. This, too, is much more easily said than done. While peer pressure is most prevalent among younger individuals, especially teenagers, it occurs among people of all age groups. Dealing with peer pressure is a classic problem that virtually everyone experiences at some point in their life. Changing one's peer group, while usually a very difficult thing to do, is frequently a workable solution. The person who has taken LSD repeatedly for a long period of time may develop the amotivational syndrome, as described earlier. A person with this problem usually needs psychotherapy to cure his problem.

One outgrowth of the drug culture has been an increased awareness of one's physical well-being, including a heightened concern with what we breathe, drink, and eat, as well as with the overall condition of the body. Running, one popular discipline, is now enthusiastically enjoyed by about 11% of all American adults.

What is really needed in all of these cases is some realistic substitute for drugs. The person must find some alternative activity to keep his mind and hands off drugs.

Physical Exercise

One frequently suggested alternative is regular exercise. Aside from the obvious physical benefits, exercise provides numerous psychological rewards. It can reduce stress, increase personal awareness, and produce a positive self-image. It has also proven helpful in alleviating depression, sleeplessness, nervousness, anxiety, and inability to cope with society. Certain types of exercise, such as jogging, can even provide a temporary escape from the hard realities of life that lead some people to drugs in the first place. A recent article in *Runner's World* stresses the point:

> *Any measurable psychological benefits from running may come not from the activity itself, but from the opportunity that act gives the runner to get away from the stresses and pressures of modern civilization. You cannot answer a jangling telephone or pay bills while circling the running track, and long runs in the woods or on back country roads may permit otherwise harassed business executives or housewives to let their minds "spin free," engage in the form of conscious daydreaming and relaxation.*

In fact, runners and others engaged in strenuous exercise frequently report a "high," or feeling of euphoria, from extreme physical exertion. The exact brain mechanism producing this effect is not known, but it is clear that the brain possesses its own mechanism for eliciting euphoria independent of any drug use. For those individuals who thoroughly enjoy social interaction, there are plenty of exercise programs that allow for this.

Another type of therapy for chronic LSD abusers has been termed the "wilderness experience." Many of these programs involve "risk recreation." This activity may be particularly attractive to the chronic LSD user who often takes the drug to experience new dimensions and who enjoys the risk of entering the unknown. One organization, called "Bridge Over Troubled Waters, Inc.," located in Berkeley, California, offers drug-users the opportunity to engage in risky adventures in place of taking drugs. Activities include parachuting, rock climbing, skin diving, and others. One participant in this program reported the following with regard to a river rafting experience: "I thought it was going to be a complete bore. But then I got on that raft, and all the way down the river I felt light; I was singing, hollering. (River running) ... provided me with natural highs and challenges to supplant those I had been getting from involvement with (drugs) ... when we finished that run I was eager to get off on more adventures. I had enjoyed the challenge of the river more than that of running the streets looking for a (drug)."

The "wilderness experiences" are in reality very safe since they are closely supervised by highly trained personnel. However, the participants feel a sense of real danger, and this gives them the high, the new experience, they are frequently seeking by taking LSD. Wilderness experiences are not for everyone, however. It must make the participant feel good. As One Bridge Over Trouble Waters consultant commented, "Dope makes you feel good, and unless you give the (users) an alternative (that does the same), it's all a lot of talk. For them there's no feeling good without (drugs). It is a meaningless abstraction until we make the abstraction real. We are saying to them, 'Hey, come do this with us, get away from the whoring and the pimping and the buying of dope, come with us and feel good, come and get high on the 'natch.' "

Meditation

For those people less inclined towards physical activities, there are other alternatives to LSD use that can provide new and exciting possibilities. One is meditation. There are several forms of meditation but probably the best known and most widely practiced form is transcendental meditation. The process of meditation was developed several thousand years ago by Indian religious leaders and philosophers. Basically, it is a form of deep physiological relaxation. The individual is taught to empty his mind of all thoughts by means of repeating certain sounds, or words, and through specific breathing techniques. To the experienced meditator this process can be very relaxing and can also provide new and exciting psychological and perceptual experiences. Experienced meditators claim they are able to reach a new level of awareness, or higher state of consciousness, through meditation. Individuals who have taken LSD in the past and have turned to meditation frequently report that the new level of consciousness they reach through meditation is far better than any LSD trip they ever experienced. And, of course, meditation does not produce toxic effects.

Brain physiologists have discovered that meditation results in "synchronized" brain waves, not unlike those observed during light sleep. Thus, the individual practicing meditation, while fully awake and alert to his internal experiences, displays external physiological signs that resemble sleep. Interestingly, LSD and other hallucinogens, including DOM, mescaline, and DMT, have been shown to produce a brain wave pattern similar to that observed in an experienced meditator.

On October 6, 1967, hundreds of San Francisco hippies gathered to participate in the parade and ceremony to mourn "The Death of the Hippie." Afterwards, Timothy Leary went on to become a stand-up comic; Michael McClure traveled around the world seeing his plays produced and his books published; and Allen Ginsberg, Gary Snyder, and Ken Kesey continued with their writing careers. Michael Bowen's daisies were last seen protruding from the rifle muzzles of soldiers outside the Pentagon.

Biofeedback

Another alternative to drugs for those less inclined towards physical activity is a process called biofeedback, in which the individual is connected to a machine that monitors various bodily processes, such as respiration, blood pressure, and heart rate. He learns to slow these processes solely through mental processes. This allows him to relax and usually to expand his consciousness and self-awareness. After a certain amount of training, an individual is often able to obtain the same results without the mechanical feedback of information from the machine. Biofeedback has been successfully used to treat many chronic LSD users, and many report that the experience derived through biofeedback is superior to that obtained with the drug.

In summary, there are various therapies for the LSD user. Acute LSD toxicity is usually treated by administration of a neuroleptic or antipsychotic drug. However, a more

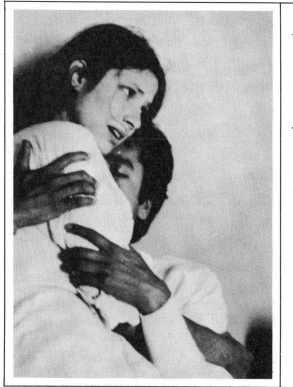

The sudden loss of the familiar effects of LSD can be compensated with the support of friendship. This may require cultivating new relationships with persons not involved with drugs or reestablishing ties with friends previously dropped because of their lack of interest in drugs. However, ultimately the abrupt change demands that the ex-LSD user be willing to accept others' sincere concern.

significant problem is the chronic LSD user. While LSD is not addicting, it can become habit-forming. In the case of the chronic LSD user, changes in self-perception and behavior are needed. Several types of therapy have been described and sometimes more than one type of therapy is needed. Some people prefer to get a high through a physical activity or risky adventures, while others prefer to concentrate on mental stimulation, which can be provided by meditation and biofeedback and/or psychotherapy. In many cases, a combination of a physical activity (exercise or risk-taking) and mental activity (meditation or biofeedback) is the best substitute for LSD use. Education is an important part of the process of rehabilitating a chronic LSD user. He must first be informed of the mental and physical consequences of chronic LSD use. Once the person realizes that he may be doing great harm to his body and mind by taking LSD and is willing to investigate alternatives to drugs, the turning point in rehabilitation has been achieved.

Biofeedback makes it possible for a person to learn how to manipulate bodily processes which were previously considered beyond conscious control. With results similar to meditation, using biofeedback can help a person deepen his relaxation and expand his consciousness.

While only humans can attempt to describe their hallucinogenic experiences, other animals willfully ingest hallucinogens. For example, the mongooses of Hawaii eat the toad Bufo marinus, *which contains a psychoactive agent. When the chimpanzee, which is evolutionarily close to humans, is given LSD, it behaves like a human on LSD.*

CHAPTER 8

HALLUCINOGENS AND THE ANIMAL KINGDOM

*M*any hallucinogenic drugs are found in nature in a variety of plants. These drugs include mescaline, psilocybin, and a form of LSD. Why are hallucinogenic compounds found in nature in the first place, and why does the human brain contain a mechanism that allows these chemicals to elicit such powerful changes in perception, mood, and behavior? To date no one has come up with a satisfactory answer to these questions. The best we can do then is speculate.

Plants that Contain Hallucinogens

The Peyote cactus, which grows wild in Mexico, Arizona, California, and Texas, contains the hallucinogenic compound mescaline. Its hallucinogenic properties have been known for centuries and extracts of the plant have long been used in religious rituals by the Aztec Indians. After ingesting the compound, users of this plant experience a period of hallucinations, accompanied by nausea and vomiting. They also have visions of kaleidoscopic fields of golden jewels.

Another variety of a naturally occurring hallucinogen found in plants is the drug psilocin, found in the mushrooms *Psilocybe mexicana*. The properties of this drug apparently have been known for centuries. Images of these mushrooms have been discovered carved into stone in Guatemala, dating back to 1000 B.C. In fact, the images are frequently formed into the shape of a god. The first recorded use of

Psilocybe in history occurred during the coronation feast of Montezuma in 1502. A counterpart of LSD that is found in nature is the plant ololiuqui, which was also used in various religious ceremonies.

It is important to realize that all of these plants containing hallucinogenic chemicals were originally used by the ancients to receive messages from and to worship their gods. In fact, these plants were frequently called the "flesh of the gods." Today LSD and related hallucinogens are rarely used in religious context and relatively few individuals report any sort of religious experience after using them. The most notable exception to this is the Native American Church, whose members have been given permission by the United States Government to continue to use mushrooms containing psilocybin in their religious ceremonies.

Animals Eat Hallucinogenic Plants

Human beings are not the only species to use hallucinogenic drugs derived from plants. Many animals consume mushrooms and cacti containing hallucinogenic chemicals. Animals can learn that certain plants are capable of producing certain effects after consumption. Thus, the animals are not taking these plants purely by accident. Though they probably initially discover the hallucinogenic properties of the plant by accident, the effects are apparently reinforcing since they return repeatedly to ingest the plant. Whether the animals experience hallucinations similar to those expe-

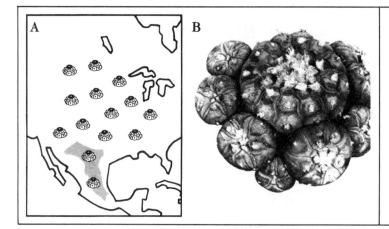

A. *Peyote use was confined to the shaded area until the 20th century, when it spread north and more than 50 American Indian tribes used it in communal ceremonies.*
B. *A peyote cluster.*

rienced by humans is another matter, but many observations of wild animals suggest that they do.

Mongooses on the Hawaiian Islands and in the West Indies eat *Bufo marinus*, a toad that contains an LSD-like hallucinogen. It is not known for certain whether this food alters the behavior of the mongoose. However, there are a large number of other species of toads that do not contain hallucinogens available, as well as other foods, but the mongoose prefers the toads containing hallucinogenic chemicals.

On the Hawaiian Islands domesticated dogs are widely used to help herd cattle. These dogs have been observed to become excessively playful after eating hallucinogenic mushrooms in the pastures. Hawaiian Island birds feed regularly on the hallucinogen-containing cactus *Trichocereus pachanoi*, and natives of the islands have reported that the birds show abnormal flight patterns after consuming the plant.

In the Asian forests, reindeer ingest the hallucinogenic mushroom *Amanita muscaria*, and their resulting behavior has been described as abnormally aggressive, loud, and intoxicated.

Many species of the cat family have been observed to consume hallucinogen-containing plants. Shortly after eating such plants, the cats display excessive sniffing, head shaking, chewing, licking, playfulness, and body rolls.

Two views of a pre-Columbian (1000-500 B.C.) stone mushroom with a kneeling young woman, used by Mayan mushroom worshippers. There were cultures whose members worshipped mushrooms as far back as 6,000 years ago.

In addition to the ingestion of plants containing halluci-nogenic compounds by animals in the wild, behavioral scien-tists have administered LSD to a wide variety of animals, including insects, fish, birds, mice, cats, dogs, and elephants. In all species tested, LSD produced hallucinatory-like, bi-zarre behavior. Thus, it appears that the brain mechanisms in humans that produce hallucinations when exposed to LSD and related drugs are present in a wide variety of animals as well.

Laboratory studies have demonstrated that pigeons given LSD show impaired visual discrimination, that is, they are no longer able to tell the difference between two objects that they could easily differentiate before LSD treatment.

When mice are given LSD their hair stands on end and they shake their heads and walk backwards. They also scratch their ears much more than normal and frequently show increased aggressiveness. Rats respond in a similar manner. In addition, mice and rats injected with LSD respond abnor-

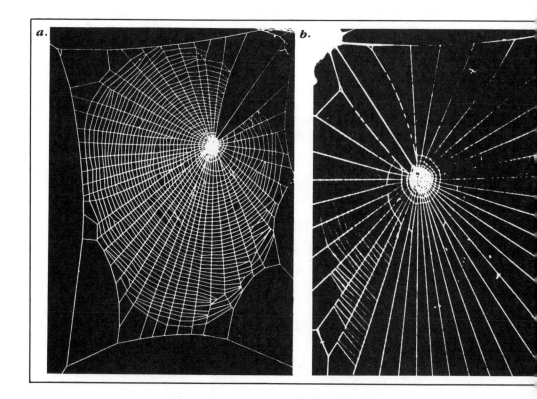

mally to sounds and objects.

Cats and dogs given LSD in the laboratory behave similar to cats that eat hallucinogen-containing plants in the wild. They chase prey that does not exist. They also adopt abnormal postures, such as sitting in a weird position with one leg extended into space. They also shake their limbs frequently, as if to remove some foreign object from their paws.

Monkeys and chimpanzees have also been tested for their response to LSD. These animals show hyperexcitability, jump about their cages as if they were trying to escape the hallucinations, and grasp at "objects" in the air when no such objects actually exist. They also scream, run backwards as if trying to escape something, and cover their eyes with both hands in a "see no evil" fashion.

From these animal studies we see that the closer the animal is to humans on the biological scale, the more their LSD-induced behavior resembles that of humans.

c. *Webs built by the spider* Zilla-x-notata Cl. *under normal conditions (a), and after ingesting LSD (b) and mescaline (c). While fewer webs were created after ingestion of the hallucinogens, the LSD webs were more regular with respect to the spokes and the spiral spacing. Interestingly, though human subjects are generally unable to differentiate between the mental effects of LSD and mescaline, the mescaline webs are markedly more irregular and abstract than those produced under the influence of LSD.*

Hallucinations and Creativity

Why do animal and human brains contain a mechanism on which the hallucinogenic compound can act so powerfully? As discussed previously, the use of LSD, particularly when used chronically, can be very toxic, even life-threatening. What is the advantage of being able to hallucinate? There is obviously no survival value, since a person on LSD or a related hallucinogen is usually incapacitated. Therefore, the mechanism in the brain by which LSD and other hallucinogenic drugs produce their characteristic psychological effects must have some other purpose. The brain clearly possesses mechanisms for related psychological experiences.

Creativity, for example, is a major part of our lives. We can close our eyes, blocking out all external sensations, and still see vivid images. In addition, while dreaming, we are able to see, hear, smell, taste, and feel "things" not actually present. Some investigators have suggested, in fact, that there is a close link between dreams and drug-induced hallucinations, and that the mechanism responsible for each is similar, if not identical. Dreams, in fact, are hallucinations of a sort. When something goes wrong with the brain mechanism responsible for drug-induced hallucinations and dreaming, there may be a spontaneous occurrence of hallucinations during waking. This may be the situation in psychotic or schizophrenic individuals. During an acute schizophrenic episode, the individual frequently experiences hallucinations similar to those that occur after LSD ingestion in a normal person. Furthermore, the usual treatment of

Drawing of Hopi god of the fields, before (left) and during an LSD trip. LSD may abstract the physical characteristics, and bring out the subjective, emotional qualities of an artist's subject.

schizophrenia, the administration of neuroleptics, is the same treatment usually administered to individuals suffering a bad LSD trip.

In short, the human brain possesses the capacity for creativity, imagination, and dreaming. When something goes wrong with this capacity, schizophrenia may sometimes occur. It may be a coincidence that LSD and related hallucinogens interefere with the normal functioning of the brain and produce hallucinations in a normal individual.

Hide-and-Seek *by Pavel Tchelitchew. While he had no exposure to psychedelic drugs, Tchelitchew's paintings illustrate the mysticism and symbolic level of consciousness often seen in LSD-induced art.*

After an LSD experience artist Harriette Frances created this graphic and wrote, "I began to feel the dissolution of my Ego, my sense of self, and fought for a time against relinquishing control of my known self to the unknown subconscious part of me, and this conflict resolved itself in my 'death'."

APPENDIX 1

HELPING A FRIEND WITH AN LSD PROBLEM

Many responses to LSD will not result in danger and are not cause for undue alarm. Hallucinations, rapid and dramatic mood changes, mixing up sight and sound, distorting time and place, and dream-like feelings are all common to an LSD experience. More extreme responses, however, can be harmful or even fatal.

Comfort, support, and protection are what the extremely panicked or anxious user needs most during a bad trip. The friend of a person experiencing extreme reactions to LSD should calm him with words of assurance and with a comfortable place where he can rest and recover. It is frequently possible to talk the user down by appealing to reason and by distracting him. His attention may be diverted by engaging in some physical activity like deep breathing, by beating time to music, or by dancing. He should never be given the opportunity to leave this environment, for a panicked user who falls into an aggressive scene away from a friend could easily harm himself or others.

If the user cannot calm down, he should be taken to a hospital emergency room where he can be given professional care. Though most people do not want to admit to using illegal drugs, it is far better to confess the problem to a doctor and receive help than to risk the dangers of nontreatment.

The three following examples might better illustrate the symptoms of acute reactions to LSD.

1. After being persuaded by his friends, a 20-year-old university student took 150 micrograms of LSD. He described his experience as being "interesting but disturbing." Afterwards he often felt that life was meaningless and he said that he was "philosophically confused." Some days he again felt normal for a few hours, but then the walls would begin to move and close in on him and time would stand still. He feared he was going crazy. Occasionally he had thoughts of self-destruction. Sometimes he would become upset and panicky, break out into a sweat, and freeze in terror. It became very difficult for him to concentrate, and he de-

cided to drop out of school. However, he was able to continue his part-time job as a stock clerk. With considerable support, strong reassurance, and tranquillizer therapy, the condition subsided six months after the LSD session. (Reported by Dr. Sidney Cohen, 1965.)

2. A 21-year-old woman and her lover were admitted to the hospital. He had had a number of LSD experiences and convinced her that taking LSD would make her less sexually constrained. About 30 minutes after ingesting approximately 200 micrograms, she noticed that the bricks in the wall had begun to fade in and out and that the light in the room seemed strange. She became frightened when she was unable to distinguish her body from the chair on which she was sitting or from her lover's body. When she began to worry that she would not get back into herself, her fear increased. At the time of admission to the hospital she was hyperactive, laughing inappropriately, and her speech was illogical. Two days later this reaction had ceased. However, because of her frightening experience she said she would never take it again. (Reported by Drs. William A. Frosch, Edwin S. Robbins, and Marvin Stern, 1965.)

3. Six months prior to her hospitalization, an attractive, single, 18-year-old female was a gregarious, popular, active, and high-achieving high school senior. At that time she began to experiment with LSD, amphetamines, and marijuana. Within months her behavior became noticeably more active, restless, and talkative. Following the ingestion of LSD at a graduation party she became sleepless, constantly active, talkative, and frequently unintelligible. Her parents sought psychiatric help and within three days she was hospitalized.

After admission an evaluation revealed that the patient was disoriented to time and place, agitated, impulsive, and hyperactive, with idiosyncratic and sexually suggestive gesturing and posturing. Her mood and behavior were unstable and inappropriate, swinging abruptly between tearful depression and laughing euphoria. Her continual stream of ideas was irrational, incoherent, and fanciful. The patient's thoughts centered on her belief that she was pregnant, in conflict with the devil, and was going to die of cancer. Auditory and visual hallucinations were also present. (Reported by Dr. Harvey A. Horowitz, 1975.)

APPENDIX 2

CASE STUDIES

This appendix contains findings from two case studies which recorded the responses of numerous LSD abusers. The first study, done in 1968, examined 21 chronic LSD abusers, measuring their character, their behavior during the LSD trip, and the aftereffects. The second study, done in 1967 and based on 21 studies and 225 cases of LSD abusers, reports the possible adverse reactions to LSD. Both studies have added to the general understanding of LSD.

Case 1

The first study reports that as a result of ingesting LSD the user becomes more sensitive to his surroundings. The individual experiences an increased awareness of colors, sounds, and textures, and objects seem brighter, louder, or fluffier. Occasionally synesthesia, or a mixing of the senses, will occur. Therefore the ringing of a telephone can turn a quiet, patterned image of pink and gray into a visual field of intense green. Thoughts may appear as pictures, and emotions may become artistic or poetic visions. For example, the user may experience emotional coldness as a recurring image of an iceberg. What was once just a chair, with LSD becomes a series of bright colors and soft shapes.

A person may no longer be able to see the difference between his feelings or thoughts and actual external events. The LSD experience depends upon the user's personality and emotions. If the emotion is love, the images and sensations may consist of tender scenes from childhood or religious themes. He forgets who he is, and instead sees himself as an inseparable part of a universe of love. Anger or hate may be magnified into a nightmare in which he falls into a world of darkness containing horrible, primitive creatures. Anger turns into images of demons that attack and destroy. The user's feelings can result in a terrifying or, if the emotion is love, wonderful experience.

These intense and powerful experiences shape an

individual's thoughts, beliefs, and behavior. Positive experiences are rewarding while negative ones can be detrimental, as described in the second study where frightened and reluctant users become more frightened and sometimes dangerous under the influence of LSD.

If, as observed in these people, it is true that LSD changes the way a person perceives things, and if it plays a major role in the creation of his emotional framework—his perception of aggression and passivity, illusion and reality—

A person using LSD may find himself suddenly surrounded by a tremendous number of nuances and details, as illustrated in Ivan Albright's Self-Portrait at 55 East Division Street. *Depending on the general quality of the LSD experience, these perceptions may either be curious and stimulating or terrifying.*

doctors argue that LSD may be helpful in treating certain types of mentally ill patients. According to this study, for example, LSD users are nonaggressive and introspective. Prior to the ingestion of LSD, these individuals were angry with their parents and with their own shortcomings. After frequent ingestions of LSD they became passive, tolerant of their parents, and preoccupied with their own inner feelings. But, as one doctor points out, many LSD users lack aggression so completely that "the tackling of a task or a problem, the self-respect without which everything that man does from morning till evening, from the morning shave to the sublimest artistic or scientific creations, would lose all impetus; everything associated with ambition, ranking order, and countless other equally indispensible behavior patterns would probably also disappear from human life." Also, because of the frequent sense of being able to use the mind to control the environment, as LSD users feel they do when they stop time and create scenes from thoughts and emotions, belief in magic and in the ability to be all-powerful increases. And this belief could lead to harmful behavier.

However, data are still conflicting. In this study, for example, electroencephalograms, or a measurement of brain waves, were taken of the LSD users, and several records showed brain wave abnormalities. One subject showed a deterioration in his performance on intelligence tests, perhaps suggesting brain damage. On the other hand, another subject who regularly took LSD on weekends exhibited brain abnormalities yet maintained an A average in junior college. Clearly much more research is necessary before firm conclusions can be made.

Case 2

The second case study focuses on the adverse reactions to LSD. Of the 225 LSD experiences studied, there were 142 cases of prolonged psychotic reactions, 63 nonpsychotic reactions, 11 flashbacks, 19 attempted suicides, four attempted homicides, 11 suicides, one homicide, and nine cases showing suicidal tendencies. There were no cases of physical drug dependency, addiction, or death due to toxic effects, but there were seven cases of convulsions.

During an LSD trip the user might suddenly be forced to confront aspects of his or her personality which are distorted and/or exaggerated. If the user is prone to psychological problems and finds him- or herself in an unsupportive setting, such a meeting might lead to terror or panic.

APPENDIX 3

REACTIONS TO LSD

Toxic Reactions

With any drug as potent as LSD there is always the possibility of deadly toxicity. When the drug is taken in small pure doses the acute toxic effects of LSD at first appear to be of minor importance. Nonetheless, there have been reports of convulsions and chromosomal damage due to LSD. Other than in those cases where people have ingested morning-glory seeds which contain LSD and a variety of other substances, there have been no reports of LSD poisoning.

Therefore, the lethal dose of LSD for humans is not known. LSD overdose in animals results in dilation of the pupils, hair standing on end, vomiting, increased reflex activity, and lack of coordination. Death results from failure to breathe.

The long-term toxic effects of LSD have not been studied in humans. Rats given a small dose of LSD for 30 days showed increased reflex responses, dilation of the pupils, hair standing on end, and a slower growth rate. Finally, the reports by a few investigators that LSD can produce convulsions are the only clear instances of a toxic response to LSD in humans, and even these are quite rare.

The typical responses to LSD include bizarre visual experiences such as a heightening of brightness and color, distortions in the perception of objects, and visual hallucinations. The emotional effects can include anxiety, panic, euphoria, or depression. Although LSD experiences were originally believed to resemble schizophrenic episodes, it is now generally accepted that the LSD experience is more personal and emotional than schizophrenic. A number of cases have been reported, however, in which LSD has produced prolonged psychotic episodes (periods of severe mental disorder and personality change). Sometimes these episodes disappear without treatment but often they must be treated with tranquillizers. In many cases they have disappeared only to reappear a few weeks later.

Of the 225 cases studied, there were 142 cases of

prolonged psychotic reactions to LSD, including those in therapeutic, experimental, and unsupervised settings. The most common symptoms were paranoia, schizophrenic-like hallucinations and extreme anxiety. Most of these required tranquillizer medication or hospitalization lasting from a few days to several years. Sixty-eight percent of 70 cases studied required more than one month in a hospital, but five to six months of hospitalization is not unusual. Psychiatrists at Bellevue Hospital in New York found that 30 of 52 patients with prolonged psychotic reactions to LSD became normal within 48 hours. Eleven other patients required two to seven days and six others required a longer period of time. Surprisingly, five of this group of six patients had no history of psychoses. Thus, it is clear that prolonged psychoses can result from LSD use.

Some people who experienced prolonged psychoses after illicit use of LSD had previous psychiatric conditions. In one study five out of 12 who had prolonged reactions had been previously diagnosed as psychotic, while the others had some personality problem. In another study 27 out of 70 persons with a combination of psychotic and nonpsychotic reactions had previous psychiatric treatment; and 25 (36%) had been diagnosed as psychotic before taking LSD. The Bellevue studies concluded that only 12 out of 52 people (23%) previously exhibited psychotic or schizoid personalities and of these, seven were able to function in society. However, these rates of pre-LSD psychoses are much higher than those found in the general public. In addition, it is not certain how many psychotics can take LSD without having a prolonged psychotic episode. In the Bellevue study about 77% of the prolonged psychoses caused by LSD could not have been predicted from previous psychotic disturbances. LSD does produce prolonged psychoses in many people who are not psychotic, have only minor personality problems, or are generally considered normal.

Additional factors associated with the occurrence of prolonged psychoses are difficult to determine. In most therapeutic cases, the dosage taken was not large, although many studies of nonmedical use did not specify the dose. About 15% in the Bellevue study and 53% in a Los Angeles study developed a prolonged psychosis after a series of doses (more than five). From 30 to 50% had a prolonged psychosis after only one LSD experience. It appears that for many people a single dose of LSD is enough to produce psychosis, especially when it is taken in unsupervised settings.

Flashbacks

Another adverse effect is the flashback. In some cases frightening hallucinations have reappeared after weeks or months of normal behavior. One patient, after 200 to 300 doses, had daily flashbacks consisting of frightening LSD experiences, and another patient had "periodic illusions" while under stress. A third patient's flashback seems to have resulted in suicide four weeks after LSD was taken.

Three doctors reported that of the 12 people who had LSD complications, three had flashbacks. Two of these people experienced a recurring loss of identity and hallucinations, one two months after taking the drug. The third had short–lived episodes of catatonia (a rigidity of the muscles which produces immobility) and visual hallucinations more than a year after last taking LSD.

In one case study a patient had spontaneous hallucinations, consisting of pleasant panels of moving light and colors, but also terrifying illusions of people decomposing in front of her. These continued for about five months after her last use of LSD.

What specifically causes flashbacks is not known. Studies have shown that LSD is rapidly absorbed and rapidly destroyed within the body. Even though the LSD itself may not be present to bring about flashbacks, some of its effects on the brain may be sufficiently long lasting to do so. Also, the connection between flashbacks and the frequency with which LSD has been taken is not clear. Of 11 persons with recurrent flashbacks, six had taken LSD numerous times—on 9, 10, 12, 15, 25, and 200 to 300 occasions. This is very frequent when compared with the people who experienced only prolonged psychoses, about half of whom had taken it only one to three times. The direct relationship between frequent ingestion of LSD and flashbacks suggests that over repeated use LSD itself or some of its effects may persist or build up sufficiently to cause, particularly under stress, a recurring experience.

Prolonged Nonpsychotic Reactions to LSD

In addition to psychoses and flashbacks, LSD has resulted in a variety of reactions which are difficult to clarify. Sixty-three cases of nonpsychotic prolonged reactions to LSD have been described and may be classified as 39 cases of acute panic or confusion, 17 cases of depression, five cases of antisocial or psychopathic behavior, one case of a "motor-excitatory state" and one case of chronic anxiety.

Most of the nonpsychotic reactions occurred in people who took LSD alone or in unsupervised settings. The doses taken were not large, except for those who had psychopathic reactions who tended to take LSD frequently or in large doses. The nonpsychotic cases are difficult to classify since only the frequencies of symptoms are given, with several symptoms possible for each person.

Panic reactions, the most frequent, include dissociation, terror, confusion, fear of going insane, and fear of not being able to return to normal. Most of these acute reactions end within a few days, but a chronic anxiety reaction has been described which required long-term psychotherapy and tranquillizers.

Pure depression is rare and is most likely to occur together with anxiety, confusion, and panic.

In some people LSD releases psychopathic personality traits which cause asocial and criminal behavior. The frequency of these reactions is small and most of them have appeared in people with asocial or psychopathic tendencies.

Suicide

Depression followed by suicide has been reported as a result of LSD use. One study of suicides questioned 62 LSD therapists. The forty-four therapists who replied had administered LSD or mescaline (another hallucinogenic drug) to 5000 people. Of these there were five attempted suicides, though four of these occurred several months after LSD was taken. Only two of these suicides were believed to be due to LSD. This rate of suicide is very small. In fact, one doctor has concluded that it is likely that LSD actually decreased the suicide rate since in such a large group of people a higher death rate by suicide would be expected.

Only two known suicides have occurred during an LSD episode. A 20-year-old student, who had frequently taken LSD with friends, jumped from a window shortly after taking an unknown dose of LSD. Six months before his death he had complained of anxiety and an inability to study, but was diagnosed as only moderately disturbed. Severe depression or suicidal behavior was not observed before his death. Until his death he stayed in school and talked of his future. In another case a young man committed suicide within a few hours of taking LSD for therapeutic purposes.

In addition to these successful suicides, two cases of accidental death which may have been suicides have been reported. In one case a young man walked into traffic shouting "halt" after he had taken LSD, and in the other case a frequent LSD user drowned after he had taken LSD alone on a beach.

Attempted suicides are serious complications of LSD use. About one-third of them occurred in people who took LSD in nonmedical settings, although a small number occurred as a result of therapy. It is difficult to attribute all of these suicides to LSD therapy, since it is typically given to disturbed persons already prone to suicide.

The dose of LSD likely to lead to an attempted suicide cannot be determined, but it may be as low as 40 milligrams for a severely disturbed person. Little is known about the frequency of suicide among persons who take LSD in unprotected settings, although the frequency for those given LSD in therapy appears to be low.

Homicide and Assault

Some persons have reacted to LSD by being extremely emotional and aggressive. In at least four people this has led to threats and in one case to a homicide.

One man who took LSD three times became grandiose for several weeks afterwards, threatened his wife with a gun and then went to live in a desert. Another man became suspicious after taking LSD for the first time. Convinced that his friends were plotting against him, he attacked them, chasing one away and severely beating the other. The beaten man later fell or was pushed out of a fourth-floor window.

The Bellevue study also reported two attempted homicides.

There is one reported case of successful homicide which occurred after treatment with LSD. A 25-year-old woman murdered her boyfriend two days after the last of five LSD sessions. While the murder was not committed during the acute effects of LSD, the desire to kill the boyfriend was expressed during one LSD session. In this patient LSD appeared to release aggressive drives and to decrease self-control. She had previously been diagnosed as a psychopathic personality with chronic alcoholism, and prior problems may have contributed to her lack of control after LSD.

Addiction and Dependence

Addiction and dependence on LSD have been mentioned as complications, though there are few indications that they actually occur. Addiction is a state of physical dependence marked by tolerance (a decreased response after repeated use) and withdrawal symptoms. Tolerance to LSD develops rapidly but also disappears rapidly. Because many volunteers for LSD studies do not wish to take the drug again, there are no studies that have examined LSD tolerance over a long period of time (e.g., several years).

There are several reports of people taking LSD for a long time. However, no cases of addiction to LSD have been reported. Also, the literature on the peyote cult among Indians contains no cases of peyote addiction. (Peyote is the cactus which contains the hallucinogen mescaline.) In fact, this supposed characteristic was used in an argument for maintaining its freedom from legal control.

Questions have also been raised about the relationship between long-term use of LSD and psychological or social damage, such as personality changes, loss of employability, deterioration of family relationships, and moral and ethical disintegration. Again, cases of use over a long period of time have rarely been reported. The only such case involved a woman who took LSD 200 to 300 times in a year. She developed a psychological dependence on it, but exhibited no withdrawal symptoms when the use of LSD was stopped.

It has been suggested that LSD may encourage users to try addictive drugs such as heroin. However, there is no evidence to support this idea since few LSD users take heroin. In all, there have been 13 reported cases of dependence on a wide variety of sedatives and amphetamines in addition to hallucinogens. Details about the use of these drugs or the order in which they were tried are not known. It may be that the use of LSD encourages experimentation with other psychoactive drugs, though there is no data to support or refute this. More in depth studies are needed.

The Basis for Unfavorable Reactions to LSD

Studies of the responses of persons who have taken LSD in unsupervised settings have not been done. To the observer, the reported cases may appear to reflect a striking social problem, but it is uncertain what proportion of the total LSD sessions results in adverse reactions.

Several conditions are associated with unfavorable reactions to LSD. Most of the reactions in every category occur most frequently in people taking LSD in unprotected settings, alone, or with others who are taking LSD. About 80% of the prolonged psychotic reactions and nearly all of the non-psychotic reactions were not related to therapeutic use. Only three of 11 flashbacks took place after therapeutic use. However, almost two-thirds of the suicidal attempts and the only successful homicide occurred in carefully protected settings.

Flashbacks and psychopathic reactions appear almost exclusively in heavy users, but many of the other reactions appear after a single moderate dose. Judging from the reactions reported so far, no one is able to guarantee a safe dose or predict which personality is certain to create only favorable reactions to LSD. There have been cases reported in which a single moderate dose of LSD has led to an extremely adverse reaction in an otherwise normal person, though this is most likely to occur in an unprotected situation. Even when other people have been with the LSD user, suicide and psychotic reactions have occurred.

The analysis of adverse reactions also contributes to knowledge of the manner in which LSD users differ from nonusers. The users appear to be primarily male students, former students, and college graduates in their early twenties.

Of 112 for whom age was stated, 82 were under 25, only five persons were older than 40, and no one was over 50 years of age. The motivations for taking LSD are not known, nor are other details about social class, life problems, or coping mechanisms.

It is likely that for the most part illicit use of LSD is an urban phenomenon, though this conclusion may be based upon the fact that most studies of adverse reactions have come from large cities. Certainly LSD is not being used only in large cities, but its connection with cities and colleges is probably not due to chance alone.

The present state of knowledge makes it difficult to determine the reasons for the use of LSD. There have been no studies concerned with the motivations of non-therapeutic LSD users who have not had complications. More sophisticated studies of the LSD-using population are required before any conclusions can be made.

Assuming that <u>something</u> interesting would occur if she drank the contents, Alice uncorked the bottle and quickly swallowed. With LSD the greatest danger is the unpredictable response of the user.

STATE AGENCIES
FOR THE PREVENTION AND TREATMENT
OF DRUG ABUSE

ALABAMA
Department of Mental Health
Division of Mental Illness and
  Substance Abuse Community
  Programs
200 Insterstate Park Drive
P.O. Box 3710
Montgomery, AL 36193
(205) 271-9253

ALASKA
Department of Health and Social
  Services
Office of Alcoholism and Drug
  Abuse
Pouch H-05-F
Juneau, AK 99811
(907) 586-6201

ARIZONA
Department of Health Services
Division of Behavioral Health
  Services
Bureau of Community Services
Alcohol Abuse and Alcoholism
  Section
2500 East Van Buren
Phoenix, AZ 85008
(602) 255-1238

Department of Health Services
Division of Behavioral Health
  Services
Bureau of Community Services
Drug Abuse Section
2500 East Van Buren
Phoenix, AZ 85008
(602) 255-1240

ARKANSAS
Department of Human Services
Office on Alcohol and Drug Abuse
  Prevention
1515 West 7th Avenue
Suite 310
Little Rock, AR 72202
(501) 371-2603

CALIFORNIA
Department of Alcohol and Drug
  Abuse
111 Capitol Mall
Sacramento, CA 95814
(916) 445-1940

COLORADO
Department of Health
Alcohol and Drug Abuse Division
4210 East 11th Avenue
Denver, CO 80220
(303) 320-6137

CONNECTICUT
Alcohol and Drug Abuse
  Commission
999 Asylum Avenue
3rd Floor
Hartford, CT 06105
(203) 566-4145

DELAWARE
Division of Mental Health
Bureau of Alcoholism and Drug
  Abuse
1901 North Dupont Highway
Newcastle, DE 19720
(302) 421-6101

DISTRICT OF COLUMBIA
Department of Human Services
Office of Health Planning and
   Development
601 Indiana Avenue, NW
Suite 500
Washington, D.C. 20004
(202) 724-5641

FLORIDA
Department of Health and
   Rehabilitative Services
Alcoholic Rehabilitation Program
1317 Winewood Boulevard
Room 187A
Tallahassee, FL 32301
(904) 488-0396

Department of Health and
   Rehabilitative Services
Drug Abuse Program
1317 Winewood Boulevard
Building 6, Room 155
Tallahassee, FL 32301
(904) 488-0900

GEORGIA
Department of Human Resources
Division of Mental Health and
   Mental Retardation
Alcohol and Drug Section
618 Ponce De Leon Avenue, NE
Atlanta, GA 30365-2101
(404) 894-4785

HAWAII
Department of Health
Mental Health Division
Alcohol and Drug Abuse Branch
1250 Punch Bowl Street
P.O. Box 3378
Honolulu, HI 96801
(808) 548-4280

IDAHO
Department of Health and Welfare
Bureau of Preventive Medicine
Substance Abuse Section
450 West State
Boise, ID 83720
(208) 334-4368

ILLINOIS
Department of Mental Health and
   Developmental Disabilities
Division of Alcoholism
160 North La Salle Street
Room 1500
Chicago, IL 60601
(312) 793-2907

Illinois Dangerous Drugs
   Commission
300 North State Street
Suite 1500
Chicago, IL 60610
(312) 822-9860

INDIANA
Department of Mental Health
Division of Addiction Services
429 North Pennsylvania Street
Indianapolis, IN 46204
(317) 232-7816

IOWA
Department of Substance Abuse
505 5th Avenue
Insurance Exchange Building
Suite 202
Des Moines, IA 50319
(515) 281-3641

KANSAS
Department of Social Rehabilitation
Alcohol and Drug Abuse Services
2700 West 6th Street
Biddle Building
Topeka, KS 66606
(913) 296-3925

KENTUCKY
Cabinet for Human Resources
Department of Health Services
Substance Abuse Branch
275 East Main Street
Frankfort, KY 40601
(502) 564-2880

LOUISIANA
Department of Health and Human
  Resources
Office of Mental Health and
  Substance Abuse
655 North 5th Street
P.O. Box 4049
Baton Rouge, LA 70821
(504) 342-2565

MAINE
Department of Human Services
Office of Alcoholism and Drug
  Abuse Prevention
Bureau of Rehabilitation
32 Winthrop Street
Augusta, ME 04330
(207) 289-2781

MARYLAND
Alcoholism Control Administration
201 West Preston Street
Fourth Floor
Baltimore, MD 21201
(301) 383-2977

State Health Department
Drug Abuse Administration
201 West Preston Street
Baltimore, MD 21201
(301) 383-3312

MASSACHUSETTS
Department of Public Health
Division of Alcoholism
755 Boylston Street
Sixth Floor
Boston, MA 02116
(617) 727-1960

Department of Public Health
Division of Drug Rehabilitation
600 Washington Street
Boston, MA 02114
(617) 727-8617

MICHIGAN
Department of Public Health
Office of Substance Abuse Services
3500 North Logan Street
P.O. Box 30035
Lansing, MI 48909
(517) 373-8603

MINNESOTA
Department of Public Welfare
Chemical Dependency Program
  Division
Centennial Building
658 Cedar Street
4th Floor
Saint Paul, MN 55155
(612) 296-4614

MISSISSIPPI
Department of Mental Health
Division of Alcohol and Drug Abuse
1102 Robert E. Lee Building
Jackson, MS 39201
(601) 359-1297

MISSOURI
Department of Mental Health
Division of Alcoholism and Drug
  Abuse
2002 Missouri Boulevard
P.O. Box 687
Jefferson City, MO 65102
(314) 751-4942

MONTANA
Department of Institutions
Alcohol and Drug Abuse Division
1539 11th Avenue
Helena, MT 59620
(406) 449-2827

NEBRASKA
Department of Public Institutions
Division of Alcoholism and Drug Abuse
801 West Van Dorn Street
P.O. Box 94728
Lincoln, NB 68509
(402) 471-2851, Ext. 415

NEVADA
Department of Human Resources
Bureau of Alcohol and Drug Abuse
505 East King Street
Carson City, NV 89710
(702) 885-4790

NEW HAMPSHIRE
Department of Health and Welfare
Office of Alcohol and Drug Abuse
   Prevention
Hazen Drive
Health and Welfare Building
Concord, NH 03301
(603) 271-4627

NEW JERSEY
Department of Health
Division of Alcoholism
129 East Hanover Street CN 362
Trenton, NJ 08625
(609) 292-8949

Department of Health
Division of Narcotic and Drug Abuse
   Control
129 East Hanover Street CN 362
Trenton, NJ 08625
(609) 292-8949

NEW MEXICO
Health and Environment Department
Behavioral Services Division
Substance Abuse Bureau
725 Saint Michaels Drive
P.O. Box 968
Santa Fe, NM 87503
(505) 984-0020, Ext. 304

NEW YORK
Division of Alcoholism and Alcohol
   Abuse
194 Washington Avenue
Albany, NY 12210
(518) 474-5417

Division of Substance Abuse
   Services
Executive Park South
Box 8200
Albany, NY 12203
(518) 457-7629

NORTH CAROLINA
Department of Human Resources
Division of Mental Health, Mental
   Retardation and Substance Abuse
   Services
Alcohol and Drug Abuse Services
325 North Salisbury Street
Albemarle Building
Raleigh, NC 27611
(919) 733-4670

NORTH DAKOTA
Department of Human Services
Division of Alcoholism and Drug
   Abuse
State Capitol Building
Bismarck, ND 58505
(701) 224-2767

OHIO
Department of Health
Division of Alcoholism
246 North High Street
P.O. Box 118
Columbus, OH 43216
(614) 466-3543

Department of Mental Health
Bureau of Drug Abuse
65 South Front Street
Columbus, OH 43215
(614) 466-9023

OKLAHOMA

Department of Mental Health
Alcohol and Drug Programs
4545 North Lincoln Boulevard
Suite 100 East Terrace
P.O. Box 53277
Oklahoma City, OK 73152
(405) 521-0044

OREGON

Department of Human Resources
Mental Health Division
Office of Programs for Alcohol and
  Drug Problems
2575 Bittern Street, NE
Salem, OR 97310
(503) 378-2163

PENNSYLVANIA

Department of Health
Office of Drug and Alcohol
  Programs
Commonwealth and Forster Avenues
Health and Welfare Building
P.O. Box 90
Harrisburg, PA 17108
(717) 787-9857

RHODE ISLAND

Department of Mental Health,
  Mental Retardation and Hospitals
Division of Substance Abuse
Substance Abuse Administration
  Building
Cranston, RI 02920
(401) 464-2091

SOUTH CAROLINA

Commission on Alcohol and Drug
  Abuse
3700 Forest Drive
Columbia, SC 29204
(803) 758-2521

SOUTH DAKOTA

Department of Health
Division of Alcohol and Drug Abuse
523 East Capitol, Joe Foss Building
Pierre, SD 57501
(605) 773-4806

TENNESSEE

Department of Mental Health and
  Mental Retardation
Alcohol and Drug Abuse Services
505 Deaderick Street
James K. Polk Building, Fourth Floor
Nashville, TN 37219
(615) 741-1921

TEXAS

Commission on Alcoholism
809 Sam Houston State Office Building
Austin, TX 78701
(512) 475-2577

Department of Community Affairs
Drug Abuse Prevention Division
2015 South Interstate Highway 35
P.O. Box 13166
Austin, TX 78711
(512) 443-4100

UTAH

Department of Social Services
Division of Alcoholism and Drugs
150 West North Temple
Suite 350
P.O. Box 2500
Salt Lake City, UT 84110
(801) 533-6532

VERMONT

Agency of Human Services
Department of Social and
  Rehabilitation Services
Alcohol and Drug Abuse Division
103 South Main Street
Waterbury, VT 05676
(802) 241-2170

VIRGINIA
Department of Mental Health and
  Mental Retardation
Division of Substance Abuse
109 Governor Street
P.O. Box 1797
Richmond, VA 23214
(804) 786-5313

WASHINGTON
Department of Social and Health
  Service
Bureau of Alcohol and Substance
  Abuse
Office Building—44 W
Olympia, WA 98504
(206) 753-5866

WEST VIRGINIA
Department of Health
Office of Behavioral Health Services
Division on Alcoholism and Drug
  Abuse
1800 Washington Street East
Building 3 Room 451
Charleston, WV 25305
(304) 348-2276

WISCONSIN
Department of Health and Social
  Services
Division of Community Services
Bureau of Community Programs
Alcohol and Other Drug Abuse
  Program Office
1 West Wilson Street
P.O. Box 7851
Madison, WI 53707
(608) 266-2717

WYOMING
Alcohol and Drug Abuse Programs
Hathaway Building
Cheyenne, WY 82002
(307) 777-7115, Ext. 7118

GUAM
Mental Health & Substance Abuse
  Agency
P.O. Box 20999
Guam 96921

PUERTO RICO
Department of Addiction Control
  Services
Alcohol Abuse Programs
P.O. Box B-Y Rio Piedras Station
Rio Piedras, PR 00928
(809) 763-5014

Department of Addiction Control
  Services
Drug Abuse Programs
P.O. Box B-Y Rio Piedras Station
Rio Piedras, PR 00928
(809) 764-8140

VIRGIN ISLANDS
Division of Mental Health,
  Alcoholism & Drug Dependency
  Services
P.O. Box 7329
Saint Thomas, Virgin Islands 00801
(809) 774-7265

AMERICAN SAMOA
LBJ Tropical Medical Center
Department of Mental Health Clinic
Pago Pago, American Samoa 96799

TRUST TERRITORIES
Director of Health Services
Office of the High Commissioner
Saipan, Trust Territories 96950

Further Reading

Barron, Frank. *LSD: Man & Society.* Westport, CT: Greenwood, 1975.

Grinspoon, Lester and Bakalar, James B. *Psychedelic Drugs Reconsidered.* New York: Basic Books, 1979.

Hofmann, Albert. *LSD—My Problem-Child.* Los Angeles: J.P. Tarcher, 1983.

Masters, R.E.L. and Houston, Jean. *Psychedelic Art.* New York: Grove Press, 1968.

Masters, R.E.L. and Houston, Jean. *The Varieties of Psychedelic Experience.* New York: Dell, 1966.

Sankar, D. Siva, et al. *LSD—A Total Study.* Westbury, NY: PJD Publications, 1975.

Stafford, Peter. *Psychedelics Encyclopedia.* Los Angeles: J.P. Tarcher, 1983.

Glossary

acid: lysergic acid diethylamide (LSD)

acid head: a regular user of LSD or other hallucinogenic substances

acid test: drug-user jargon referring to a party at which someone has added LSD to the punch bowl

acute toxicity: the short-term harmful effects of a drug

amotivational syndrome: lack of interest in everything except taking drugs

amphetamines: drugs that stimulate or excite the nervous system

analgesia: insensitivity to pain without loss of consciousness

bad trip: unwanted experience from taking LSD or another hallucinogen

biofeedback: a process of gaining control over bodily functions such as blood pressure, heart rate, respiration, and muscle tension by using information provided by a special instrument which is connected to the body

bummer: a bad trip (experience) with LSD or another hallucinogen

catatonia: a state of rigidity of the muscles which produces immobility

cerebral cortex: the most highly developed part of the brain where thinking occurs

chronic toxicity: harmful effects of a drug that last for a long time

consciousness-raising: the process of becoming more aware of the environment as well as one's own inner feelings

co-pilot: a person who takes LSD at the same time as another person

delusionogen: a drug that produces a false impression of the environment

DMT: dimethyltryptamine, an LSD-like drug

depersonalization: a feeling of being outside oneself and observing one's behavior, rather than actually experiencing it

derealization: a feeling that what one is experiencing is not actually happening but is a dream

drug culture: a nationwide group of people who regularly take illegal drugs

electroencephalogram: brain wave pattern

euphoria: a mental high characterized by a sense of feeling good

flashback: the spontaneous reoccurrence of an LSD experience

freaking out: experiencing a bad reaction to LSD

flying: experiencing the maximal effects of LSD or some other hallucinogen

good trip: a pleasurable experience with LSD or some other hallucinogen

grand mal seizure: severe convulsions with gross muscle spasms and loss of consciousness

ground control: a friend who prevents an LSD user from hurting himself

guru: an experienced LSD user

hallucination: a sensory impression that has no basis in reality

hallucinogen: a drug that produces hallucinations

joint: a marijuana cigarette

LSD: lysergic acid diethylamide

mania: mental and physical overactivity

mescaline: an hallucinogenic drug found in certain cacti, chemically similar to amphetamine

mimosa: a plant containing the hallucinogen DMT used by South American Indians to produce hallucinogenic snuffs

narcotic: a drug, such as morphine or heroin, that decreases brain activity and reduces pain

neuroleptic: a drug used to treat schizophrenia and acute LSD overdose

ololiuqui: a plant that contains a drug similar to LSD

opiate: any of a number of drugs produced from the opium poppy, such as morphine and codeine

paranoid schizophrenia: a mental disorder in which the person feels that everyone is trying to hurt him

peyote cactus: a plant that contains mescaline and is used legally by certain American Indians for religious and medical purposes

phantasticum: a drug that produces hallucinations

phencyclidine: PCP or angel dust

piptadenia: a plant containing DMT used by South American Indians to produce hallucinogenic snuffs

psilocin: an LSD-like hallucinogen

Psilocybe mexicana: a mushroom that grows in Mexico and the United States and contains the LSD-like halluci-nogen psilocybin

psilocybin: an LSD-like drug that is converted to psilocin in the body

psychedelic: producing hallucinations or having mind-altering or mind-expanding properties

psychoactive drug: a chemical that changes mood, behavior, or thought processes

psychosis: an emotional disorder with derangement of the personality and loss of contact with reality

psychotomimetic: a drug that produces psychoses

recreational drug: a chemical substance that is taken for pleasure, usually in a social gathering

risk recreation: hobbies involving danger, such as rock climbing, river rafting, and parachuting

schizophrenia: a mental disorder characterized by a loss of contact with reality

scopolamine: a drug with mild hallucinogenic properties

sedative-hypnotics: drugs that produce relaxation, relief from anxiety, and sleep

social drug: a chemical that is taken at parties for the purpose of recreation

STP: an LSD-like hallucinogen (synthetic) that is chemi-cally similar to amphetamine

synesthesia: a mixing of the senses which occurs under the influence of LSD

telekinesia: moving objects by mental powers

therapeutic: having medical or healing use

tolerance: decreased response to a drug after repeated usage

toxicity: harmful effects on the body

transcendental meditation: a type of natural relaxation and mind-expanding process developed in India and used as a substitute for LSD and other drugs

travel agent: a street drug dealer, especially of LSD and other hallucinogens

trip: an LSD experience

virola: a plant containing DMT used by South American Indians to produce hallucinogenic snuffs

Index

Michael E. Trulson received his Ph.D. in biopsychology from the University of Iowa. He has been a research associate and lecturer in the Program in Neuroscience and director of the Neurochemistry Lab at Princeton University. Currently he is associate professor of anatomy at Texas A & M University College of Medicine. He has published more than 100 research reports on psychoactive drugs in numerous scientific journals.

Solomon H. Snyder, M.D., Ph.D., is Distinguished Service Professor of Neuroscience, Pharmacology and Psychiatry at The Johns Hopkins University School of Medicine. He has served as president of the Society for Neuroscience and in 1978 received the Albert Laster Award in Medical Research. He has authored *Uses of Marijuana, Madness and the Brain, The Troubled Mind, Biological Aspects of Mental Disorder,* and edited *Perspective in Neuropharmacology: A Tribute to Julius Axelrod.* Professor Snyder was a research associate with Dr. Axelrod at the National Institute of Health.

Barry L. Jacobs, Ph.D., is currently a professor in the program of neuroscience at Princeton University. Professor Jacobs is author of *Serotonin Neurotransmission and Behavior* and *Hallucinogens: Neurochemical, Behavioral and Clinical Perspectives.* He has written many journal articles in the field of neuroscience and contributed numerous chapters to books on behavior and brain science. He has been a member of several panels of the National Institute of Mental Health.

Jerome H. Jaffe, M.D., formerly professor of psychiatry at the College of Physicians and Surgeons, Columbia University, has been named recently Director of the Addiction Research Center of the National Institute on Drug Abuse. Dr. Jaffe is also a psychopharmacologist and has conducted research on a wide range of addictive drugs and developed treatment programs for addicts. He has acted as Special Consultant to the President on Narcotics and Dangerous Drugs and was the first director of the White House Special Action Office for Drug Abuse Prevention.

DATE DUE

JUN 13			
OCT - 3 1997			